About this book

The trafficking of women and girls for the purpose of prostitution is big business. It is one of the most lucrative industries in the world, particularly given the explosion of the sex industry since the 1990s. The collapse of the Soviet Union and the devastating impact of neoliberal economic policies in many parts of the world have resulted in significant numbers of women seeking income however they can. Some women and girls suffer conditions of extreme exploitation and abuse, having little or no control over their lives. Invisible to most, many women work out of small apartments, nightclubs and hotels, trapped by debts and blackmailed by their exploiters. Increasing numbers of women are forced to compete for work in conditions of extreme sexual exploitation, often being exposed to risky sexual practices, the danger of HIV infection, violence and murder. As in many other contexts, the laws of the marketplace are applied with extreme brutality.

This book draws on a wealth of new empirical data: case studies from several countries of origin, transit and destination; research produced by NGOs, police and criminal courts; interviews and field research with the women themselves. Monzini's primary aim is to identify the mechanisms of what has truly become a global market. Most important, she assesses recent attempts to control trafficking, and strategies for resistance and change.

About the author

PAOLA MONZINI is a sociologist with a Ph.D. in social and political science from the European University Institute. She has worked as a consultant for both the Direzione Investigativa Antimafia, the Italian law enforcement agency fighting organized crime, and, more recently, as a researcher in the United Nations Interregional Crime and Justice Research Institute (UNICRI). Monzini's primary research interests are the social and political aspects of transnational organized crime, illegal markets and migration issues. This is her second book.

Sex Traffic

Prostitution, Crime and Exploitation

PAOLA MONZINI

Translated by Patrick Camiller

White Lotus
Bangkok

Fernwood Publishing
Nova Scotia

SIRD
Kuala Lumpur

David Philip
Cape Town

ZED BOOKS
London & New York

Il mercato delle donne was first published in Italy by Donzelli Editore, Rome, 2002, English-language rights by arrangement with Eulama Literary Agency, Rome

Sex Traffic was published in 2005 by

In Burma, Cambodia, Laos, Thailand and Vietnam:
White Lotus Co. Ltd, GPO Box 1141, Bangkok 10501, Thailand

In Canada: Fernwood Publishing Ltd, 8422 St Margaret's Bay Road (Hwy 3)
Site 2A, Box 5, Black Point, Nova Scotia, BOJ 1BO

In Malaysia: Strategic Information Research Development (SIRD),
No. 11/4E, Petaling Jaya, 46200 Selangor

In Southern Africa: David Philip (an imprint of New Africa Books),
99 Garfield Road, Claremont 7700, South Africa

In the rest of the world: Zed Books Ltd, 7 Cynthia Street, London N1 9JF, UK,
and Room 400, 175 Fifth Avenue, New York, NY 10010, USA
www.zedbooks.co.uk

Designed and typeset in Monotype Jansen
by illuminati, Grosmont, www.illuminatibooks.co.uk
Cover designed by Andrew Corbett
Printed and bound in the EU by Cox & Wyman, Reading

Distributed in the USA exclusively by Palgrave Macmillan, a division of
St Martin's Press, LLC, 175 Fifth Avenue, New York, NY 10010

A catalogue record for this book is available from the British Library
Library of Congress Cataloging-in-Publication Data is available

Library and Archives Canada Cataloguing in Publication
Monzini, Paola, 1965–
Sex traffic : prostitution, crime and exploitation / Paola Monzini.
Translation of: Il mercato delle donne.
Includes bibliographical references and index.
ISBN 1–55266–179–2
1. Prostitution. 2. Women–Crimes against. I. Title.
HQ281.M6613 2005   364.15´34   C2005-904247-8

ISBN 1 84277 624 x Hb (Zed Books)
ISBN 1 84277 625 8 Pb (Zed Books)

Contents

Foreword

I first met Paola Monzini at a conference on human trafficking in 1999. The conference reflected the early evolutionary stage of our understanding of modern trafficking at that time, in the strangely disorganized nature of the discussions. Everyone agreed that human trafficking was a 'bad thing', but what it was exactly, where it happened, and what should be done about it, were all up for grabs. Few if any estimates of the extent of trafficking were offered. Perhaps the greatest achievement of the conference was to help crystallize questions rather than supply answers.

Striking up a conversation with Paola Monzini, I soon found that I had managed to fall into discussion with the very person who was best able both to explain the complexities of the Italian response to its own trafficking problems and to point to the few clear answers to thorny research questions that did exist. Paola told me about the 'Nigerian woman problem' as many Italian politicians and journalists called it – the trafficking of women into prostitution from West Africa. We also began to discuss the more important side of that coin – what we now know as the 'Italian man problem' – the widespread demand for prostitution by Italian men that fuels human trafficking.

Since 1999 Paola Monzini has devoted herself to gaining a deeper understanding of trafficking of women into prostitution. We are all in her debt, because this understanding is important for a number of reasons, as it can help shape policy and practice that will prevent people being caught up in human trafficking, as well as point to ways in which those who are trapped might be helped to free themselves.

As with many criminal activities, our understanding of human trafficking is piecemeal and often based on anecdotal information. Our understanding is also complicated by the global reach of trafficking, and by social and cultural variation in the ways that the crime of trafficking unfolds. Compared to other criminal activities it is especially difficult to get a clear picture of human trafficking. In part, this is because the victims of trafficking are more likely to be hidden or unreachable than, for example, the victims of burglary, or even murder. The result is a crime for which the technique of representative sample victim surveys does not apply. This invisibility has an impact on our understanding of the demand for trafficked persons as well. Trafficking, enslavement, forced prostitution, and kidnapping share the distinction that they are crimes in which the victim is also the money-making 'product' of the criminal enterprise. Like the bag of cocaine that a trafficker also keeps hidden at all costs, the trafficking victim/product will be used and, in all likelihood, exhausted and disposed of. This fact, that the victim is also the product, makes the study of trafficking both difficult and essential. When people are products it is also crucial that we come to understand the context and reasoning behind the demand for trafficking victims.

A cool and careful investigation on which to base this understanding is doubly important because of the heated nature of the debate around the issue of prostitution. Sadly, two highly polarized camps have developed, both working against trafficking into prostitution. It sometimes seems that they devote as much energy to attacking each other as they do to helping the victims of trafficking. The fight between these two camps is long on rhetoric and short on information. Here Monzini does everyone a service: she collects facts and interprets them as honestly and calmly as she can. Yes, she has a position on this argument, but it is one she is willing to discuss and test – which is the only way this argument will ever be resolved.

If this book is an important step towards a foundation of knowledge on human trafficking, it also helps us by pointing to those areas where we are still suffering in woeful ignorance. To target anti-trafficking activities and resources better, research is needed in geographical regions where forced labour trafficking cases are emerging, on companies that profit from the flow of the products of forced labour into their product supply chains, and on those economic sectors in which there is a tendency for trafficking and forced labour to occur. These sectors include not only prostitution and pornography but also domestic services, agriculture, factory production, meatpacking, restaurant and hotel services, and warehousing and shipping. At present there is little understanding of the elasticity of demand for trafficked and forced labour in different economic sectors.

Further research on the needs and experiences of survivors is also needed. This is clear in the lack of reliable data on the health status of trafficking survivors. Future research should identify the precise health and medical consequences of trafficking: the nature of the maladies and their duration, the best practices to identify and administer services to survivors, and the level of recovery to be expected following treatment. This information should be used to develop screening protocols to help health-care professionals identify pre-existing or potential health problems. Research should be conducted to determine what kinds of follow-up health care would be needed for survivors who choose to return to their countries of origin. Researchers should solicit the active participation of survivors so that future programmes will meet the needs of survivors from diverse cultural backgrounds.

While this list of research needs is extensive, it also points to the significance of Paola Monzini's work. We are now engaged in the fourth major wave of anti-slavery and anti-trafficking work in human history. This latest wave is in its early moments, swelling and gathering strength. The shape of the wave in fifty years' time will be determined, in part, by those who took part in its birth, who saw a problem invisible to most eyes, and who let loose their curiosity and intellect to pursue that problem. Every drop that is added to this wave is important because we stand at a historical moment when, if sufficient resources and brainpower are applied, we can rid the world of slavery and trafficking for good.

Kevin Bales
Free the Slaves, Washington DC

Introduction

Elina is 19 years old, and she sees no opportunities in her home town in Ukraine. A year after the death of her father she cannot find a job, and feels alone. Sonya, the cousin of a friend, who has just spent three months in Italy, tells her about her good time there as a waitress, and introduces Elina to some men who are able to arrange documentation and travel. Elina arrives in Italy via Romania and Hungary. The trip by bus is fine, and as soon as she arrives in Milan a driver picks her up. Elina is taken to a flat in another city, where two men and two Albanian women are living. Here her feelings change dramatically. One of the men tells her that her travel debts have to be repaid, and he confiscates her documents. After repeated beatings and psychological torture, including threats to her family, she is soon forced into work as a street prostitute, like the other two women. In Verona, she is obliged to service between ten and twenty clients a night, though she speaks not a word of Italian. For weeks she is prevented from communicating with her family and she feels completely isolated. She never has a day off and receives in payment only a mattress, food and clothing.[1]

Elina's life in Italy is quite different from those of many other prostitutes. Prostitutes generally have money of their own and the ability to reject or bargain with customers; they are free to move around as they please. Elina, as all the women who have fallen prey to traffickers, has no such margin of autonomy: she can end her day, or night, only after she has collected a fixed sum – otherwise there is a beating, or a fine. She can't go out for a walk; she may be moved overnight to another country or sold to the highest bidder. She receives no remuneration for her work as she has to repay a debt. She can be subjected at any moment to physical or mental violence. She may be forced to work on the street or in closed premises such as nightclubs, video bars or massage parlours, always prone to threats and blackmail. Her exploited condition is due not to the nature of the services demanded of her but to her lack of control over her own existence.

Trafficking in human beings is not limited to prostitution: it also lies hidden in correspondence marriages and provides the material for different kinds of labour market. Millions of people around the world are its victims – in particular, women and children. Most of these 'new slaves' are socially uprooted migrants who, having moved to another country without any form of protection, find themselves saddled with debt and oppressed by extreme exploitation. Their numbers have hugely increased over the last decade.[2] In various parts of the world they may be engaged in agricultural and pastoral activity or artisanal workshops, as well as in factory labour. We shall not examine here these forms of new slavery, nor the trafficking in children for use by paedophiles, nor the pimping of transsexuals and men in the prostitution markets. The object of our research is trafficking for the female prostitution market and the forms of exploitation associated with it. This flow is sustained by adult women as well as under-age girls, who are inserted into the same cycle of exploitation and intended for the same kind of customer. Thus, since women and girls are considered in the market to be interchangeable goods, we shall use the words 'woman' and 'girl' without distinction – never forgetting, however, the greater gravity of any direct exploitation of minors.

For a number of years, newspapers, magazines and television programmes in many countries around the world have been exposing the terrible realities of the so-called 'female slave trade', including atrocious injuries inflicted on women's bodies, such as iron or cigarette burns and broken limbs. Murder is a frequent occurrence, yet many of the bodies are hidden and never discovered.

Spurning sensationalism, our research has sought to show the mechanisms that underlie the traffic in women and other forms of living off prostitution that have spread along with it. This has meant going beyond the victim/slave-master polarity and inserting the problem into a broader framework of international migration, organized crime, gender issues and the 'global' sex market.

Before we enter into our subject, let us recall that trafficking for the purposes of prostitution is not a new issue: a similar problem appeared in the late nineteenth and early twentieth centuries, when it was known as the 'white slave trade'. This expression referred to the trafficking of young women to work in conditions of semi-slavery in the far-flung brothels of the Western colonies and the great cities of the age. As today, the trade supplied mainly, but not only, the cheaper prostitution markets. It developed at a time when women and men were experiencing with especial severity the effects of widespread and rapid socio-economic change. The second industrial revolution, with its potential to destroy existing economies and societies, was forcing them to migrate in their thousands to try their luck abroad or in the major cities. In South America and Southeast Asia, for instance, a large influx from Europe was giving rise to huge concentrations of men with 'urgent' sexual needs, and hence to a growing demand for prostitution.

To correlate the labour supply of migrant women (who usually fended for themselves, without any protection) with the demand for paid sex, traffickers organized their transport to brothels in Saigon or Buenos Aires, Calcutta or Alexandria. Flows of women began from the poorer areas of Central Europe to such destinations as Turkey and Japan: we know, for example, that thousands of Czech 'harp players', as they were known, were sold to distant markets in the Far East (Butterwek 1999). The 'human flesh markets' acquired their supplies from all over Europe, following a similar dynamic. In most cases, lies about the nature of the work were used to recruit local girls, who were then taken on long and difficult journeys to the major ports and put on board steamers for destinations across the ocean. Marseilles, the European port with the largest number of transit passengers in the late nineteenth century, became the main hub of this traffic. And it was the proceeds of this 'white slave trade' which in the early twentieth century spawned a rich and powerful sector of organized crime (Monzini 1999). Alexandria was another important Mediterranean crossroads for this traffic, while Hamburg and Rotterdam became the strategic ports for northern Europe.

Other routes developed wholly inside Europe – from Britain to the continent, for example. Girls would be lured in England by newspaper advertisements offering them employment as domestic servants, or else approached at railway stations as soon as they arrived in a continental city. In 1880 the English feminist movements hired a London lawyer, T.W. Snagge, to carry out a thorough investigation into such practices, and his results showed that some of the girls recruited in these ways were taken to brothels in Belgium, the Netherlands and France, where they were harshly treated and forced to prostitute themselves against their will (Barry 1979). Only at the turn of the century did the prostitution racket capture the political attention of Europe. In

1899 an International Bureau for the Suppression of the Traffic in Persons came into being, and in 1902 the term 'white slave trade' was officially adopted at a conference in Paris that brought together representatives from various countries to draft a common document. In 1921 the League of Nations replaced it with the term still in use today: 'trafficking in women and children'.[3]

The focus on 'whites' did not actually reflect the global dimension of the phenomenon. By the late nineteenth century, the trafficking business had reached a higher level of sophistication in China than in the West (Jaschok and Miers 1994). Run by criminals who already had good international connections, the racket supplied young women to regions with a rapidly expanding population, most notably the colonies of Hong Kong and Singapore. It has been documented that only a minority of women left of their own free will: the great majority were kidnapped, tricked or handed over by their own family to 'middlemen'. In Singapore, where the population quadrupled between 1880 and 1920 and the ratio of men to women was 14:1, most of the new immigrants were coolies who toiled in the factories, built roads and palaces or loaded and unloaded goods. The prostitution market grew at a dizzying rate, so that by the turn of the century it was one of the most lucrative businesses in the colony; the picture was similar in Hong Kong. The two cities became not only destinations in themselves but also places of transit for the prostitution traffic to other regions; highly profitable networks linked the deep interior of China to cities in the US with large Chinese communities. At the beginning of the twentieth century, the price that a recruiter paid for a young woman varied between $20 and $50 in China, or $150 and $500 in Singapore, whereas brothel-owners in San Francisco had to pay anywhere between $1,500 and $3,000 to take possession of her (Barry 1979: 35). The racket, involving the total dependence and submission of girls trapped in precise mechanisms of debt and blackmail, met with a high degree of tolerance on the part of official institutions. Later, in the 1930s, the scale of the trade was visibly reduced, following important social-economic changes in the region and direct intervention by the authorities.

Some features of today's prostitution traffic mimic those of the late nineteenth century. The flows begin in economically underdeveloped areas and end in the richest markets. Although the geographical locations may have changed, the methods of recruitment have remained the same, and the traffic in women, like a hundred years ago, mainly follows the laws of profit and forms part of a wider prostitution market.

In order to understand how this market operates today, we need to consider three factors in particular: the supply, the demand and the social context in which the two intersect. In Chapter 1, which deals with the supply side, we focus on recent trends in prostitution markets and the changing attitude of customers and cultures to prostitution. Brief mention will be made here of 'sex tourism' and the role of the Internet. We shall see that, under the pressure of female migration, local markets have become more and more favourable for the customer, as the women and girls who prostitute themselves are ever younger and more attractive, and the prices charged for their services are always very moderate. We shall also see that the global prostitution market has developed in such a way that it fits in well with the supply routes of the traffic in women.

Chapter 2 examines the women's experience of migration: the roots of their desire and need to leave, the forms of migration, and the types of encounter that irregular emigration tends to involve. Here we try to reconstruct how expectations are gradually dashed and overturned, so that women in search of economic or social emancipation are trapped into situations of veritable imprisonment, and subjected to mental and physical violence of unbearable intensity that inevitably leads to changes in their personality.

To explain this trajectory in full, Chapter 3 then turns to those who live off the earnings of prostitution and to the ways in which criminal networks, often also run by foreigners, control the trade. Here we show that traffickers do not need to invest much to break into the racket and that there is little danger of being arrested – and the prospects of making a handsome profit are very promising. Analysis of a few routes will allow us to study the formation of a sector of organized crime that lives off the earnings of prostitution. It emerges that the criminal networks are not alone in drawing high profits from the exploitation of women. The wealth generated by female prostitution serves in various ways to enrich other people in the women's home countries and the lands to which they are sent. Chapter 4 looks at some of the solutions to the problem that have been proposed in the countries of origin and arrival, as well as those epilogues in which the women's journey ends with forced repatriation.

Each of the four chapters emphasizes the point of view of those who contribute to shaping the phenomenon, whether as customers, women, pimps or traffickers, or finally as institutions and non-governmental organizations opposing, or seeking to mitigate the effects of, the prostitution racket.

I would like to thank all those who, in one way or another, accompanied me in the task of uncovering the world of women trapped by the prostitution traffic. It was a difficult task, especially at the beginning. I started my investigations as a researcher at UNICRI, the United Nations Interregional Crime and Justice Research Institute. My work with Cristina Talens and Monika Peruffo, who have become dear friends, was highly stimulating. I also have pleasant memories of working with Burkhard Dammann, Meguni Takahashi and Cristina Kangaspunta at the United Nations Office on Drugs and Crime in Vienna, Fiona David and Winnie Sorgdrager, as well as Alexis Aronowitz, with all of whom I shared a common interest and passion in so many parts of the work.

In the course of three years, countless victims of the prostitution traffic and experts from various countries recounted their personal experiences, enabling me to develop a more rounded framework for study of the problem; my deepest gratitude to them all. For the sections dealing with Italy, which required the reading of court and police records, I have to thank a number of people who kindly offered me important material and suggestions: Francesco Carchedi, Cataldo Motta, Francesco Mandoi, Licia Scagliarini, Viki, Marco Bufo, Carmen Bertolazzi, Giorgio Stefano Manzi, Roberto Zuliani, Teresa Albano, Giovanni Melillo, Marco Favale and Alessia Altamura. Heartfelt thanks are also due to Monica Massari, Stefano Becucci and Ferruccio Pastore, with whom I had profitable exchanges of material and ideas. I am deeply grateful to Daniela Bassani and Luca Guzzetti, very dear friends as well as attentive readers and commentators on the Italian version of this book. Finally, a special note of thanks to Keith Sartin, whom I value as an angel and who paved the way for the English translation, and to Anna Hardman, my editor at Zed Books.

Notes

1. The story was collected in Rome, in July 2004.
2. For a general overview of the phenomenon, see Bales 1999a.
3. In 1926 the Geneva Slavery Convention redefined the slave trade to include 'all acts involved in the capture, acquisition or disposal of a person with intent to reduce him to slavery; all acts involved in the acquisition of a slave with a view to selling or exchanging him; all acts of disposal by sale or exchange of a slave acquired with a view to being sold or exchanged, and, in general, every act of trade or transport in slaves'.

The global sex market

The cultural setting

Some notes on the customers

Prostitution is a growing phenomenon, but its scale cannot be estimated with any precision: it is the kind of activity that mostly occurs in places discreetly shielded from view. So far as Europe is concerned, the number of people who regularly prostitute themselves has been put at 300,000 in Germany, whereas in Italy it is thought to be around 50,000, in a proportion of 1:1,200 inhabitants. In the Netherlands and Britain the ratio is 1:700 inhabitants. All these figures are obviously very rough: calculations based on what is visible can only tell part of the story, and the scale of street prostitution varies greatly from country to country. In London, where prostitutes mainly operate behind closed doors, the number of street customers is estimated at 7,620 a week (Home Office 2004). In Milan, a much smaller city where street activity is much more widespread, the equivalent figure is around 7,000 every evening; to be more precise, the total number of street encounters between customers and female prostitutes (excluding homosexuals, transsexuals and transvestites) has been put at 147,000 a month (Leonini 1999: 30).

It is not easy to understand the reasons why prostitution is such a massive presence in our sexually 'liberated' society. The usual explanation is that demand is created by the market supply, or by the availability of young women and girls, mainly from foreign countries, to work as prostitutes. No doubt these young and mostly beautiful immigrants, who offer themselves at affordable prices, provide a major boost to consumption. Men are attracted to them: customers ready to grasp new opportunities gladly accept commodification of the sexuality of women and girls. But to reduce everything to this is to give a purely biological reading of the customers' behaviour, based on the supposed 'irrepressibility' of the male sexual impulse in relation to women. We would rather stress the fact that, even if the deepest mechanisms of sexuality and desire are unintelligible, the widespread male orientation to commercial sex is not so obviously part of men's nature.

More interesting are those readings in which prostitution appears not simply as a solution to the physical problem of male urges, but as a reflection of the problem of relations between men and women, which has arisen from the redefinition of gender in our society. In this light, the spread of prostitution is one of the effects of recent changes in relations between the sexes. It has been argued, for example, that it constitutes a special sphere in which men unsure of their capacity for relations with the opposite sex can escape what they feel as a burden of responsibility. Although it certainly does not apply in every case, this interpretation deserves to be taken seriously, for recourse to commercial sex often can be seen as a kind of revenge or reaffirmation, however temporary, of men over women. Moreover, according to expert studies, the end of the era of female subordination – which means that women no longer correspond to the classical stereotypes – lies at the root of the success of transsexuals and transvestites; sex 'between men' makes it possible to avoid questioning male domination and gender hierarchies (Weltzer-Lang, Barbosa and Mathieu 1994).

More straightforwardly: to go with a prostitute may be experienced as a kind of 'time out', which allows a man to keep the sexual relationship as simple as possible and to escape the possibility of rejection. We find examples of this in a fascinating survey that Carla Corso, herself a prostitute and founder of the Italian Movement for the Civil Rights of Prostitutes, conducted through interviews with customers. One man in his forties told her:

> What I liked most was the male-chauvinist aspect of being able to choose without being rejected – apart from the athletics themselves, which in the end are not such an important part of the ritual. It was great choosing like a feudal lord, and being absolutely sure you wouldn't be rejected by the other person.

Or a graduate executive:

> I go with these girls because I've been pushed into it by the feminist fashion that's demolished traditional male–female relations. It makes me prefer a simple economic negotiation over the price of a service, instead of getting involved in relations that are either too cerebral (and therefore turn me off sexually) or too physical (and therefore expose my great limits as a male).... It's better to pay and let it hang out, not to have ties of any kind.... Women's demands have grown and grown; they've become more and more difficult and complicated for us men. (Corso and Landi 1998: 67)

Travel to faraway places may greatly assist the search for 'islands' in which men can defend – or at least have the illusion of defending – the status of male superiority in the face of women's social skills and growing qualifications. The purchase of sex in a foreign land can allow a man to take a real holiday, to be 'king' at least for a week. One company representative in his forties who had been to Thailand reported: 'I found a very pretty girl and – it's an ugly word – hired her for a week.... Choosing no longer came into it, but there was the pleasure of having her as a servant, not so much as a woman' (Leonini 1999: 52).

Seen in this way, commercial sex is a kind of escape from over-complicated relations. But, especially in low-priced prostitution, it is certainly not an escape that takes anyone very far. The relationship with a prostitute is something different, not homologous but parallel to other sexual experiences. Anyone who has been with a prostitute knows that, although sexual desire is the basis of the contract, it is the contract that ends up imposing its terms: the desire has to be squeezed and forced into its limits (O'Connell Davidson 1998). As one prostitute put it, the sexuality that customers express in the monetary relationship, especially in the cheaper parts of the trade, 'is a possessive sexuality, without any interchange; the aim is to reach orgasm and that's it. [Customers] don't even know what eroticism is about' (Corso and Landi 1998: 19).

It is true that – as many studies emphasize (O'Connell Davidson 1998; Seabrook 1996) – sex tourism centres on places like bars or clubs, where the girls are not seen as prostitutes in the traditional sense, and where their customers try hard to kid themselves that they are striking up a 'girlfriend' type of relationship. In the cheaper sectors back home, however, the opposite is usually the case. Customers pick up street girls in their car, or go to places where they are given only a few minutes to do their business; there are even small hotels that rent out rooms not for an hour but for five minutes.

The briefness of the encounter tells us that the sexual service is hurried, that customer and prostitute usually do not even have time to exchange a few words. More generally, the contract binding the customer to a foreign woman has a number of peculiarities:

to buy sexual services from someone who does not speak your language, and who has a lower social status and therefore less contractual power, is different from contracting the same services from skilled professionals. Interviews with clients from various parts of the world have shown that quite a lot describe foreign prostitutes as cheaper and more malleable than others, and, above all, that it is easier to have a degree of control over them which offers a good 'return' for the money (Anderson and O'Connell Davidson 2003: 21–2).

There is some dispute about this, however. Customers interviewed in Denmark place local prostitutes at the top of their hierarchy of preferences, on the grounds that, unless they are drug addicts, the services they provide are better than those of foreign women. Like their counterparts in Thailand, for example, Danish customers evaluate prostitutes on the basis of the qualities they offer: cleanliness, ability to speak the same language, care for themselves and a degree of professionalism. Prostitutes are also graded along a precise social scale: those who have been forced into prostitution by others, or by material necessity, are less attractive than those who seem to do it out of choice and enjoy better working conditions (Anderson and O'Connell Davidson 2003: 21–2). According to the same studies, if a customer deliberately chooses an immigrant woman whose market position suggests that she was forced into prostitution, this means that he does not consider the prostitute as a subject capable of entering into a contract, but rather as an object or commodity to be bought and sold for a specified time. In practice, what the customer acquires is a temporary right of possession over her. Some men admit that they seek out women in difficulty, who have been sapped by psychological wounds and extreme loneliness. As one respondent said: 'Actually, they have no one to turn to except their clients. So, many women who come from other countries get their human warmth from clients' (Indian brick kiln owner, married, aged 48) (Anderson and O'Connell Davidson 2003: 25). Another possibility is that the customer sees prostitution as a market in which women sell themselves and violence can even be justifiable. As a 54-year-old Indian bank employee put it:

> When there is violence, it is mostly the prostitute's fault. See, I am going to buy something. If I am satisfied with what I am buying, why should I be violent? I will be violent when I am cheated, when I am offered a substandard service, when I am abused or ill treated. Sometimes [violence] is because the prostitute wants the client to use a condom. They force it on the client.... He will be naturally disgruntled, and there will be altercations. (Anderson and O'Connell Davidson 2003: 24) .

This evidence confirms Julia O'Connell Davidson's view (1998) that part of the prostitution market is based on the customer's wish to have total control over another body, another person. It is a part of the market where the woman who prostitutes herself has no power over the contract underlying the client–prostitute relationship. In short, there are two contrasting positions: on the one hand, customers who prefer elective prostitutes and are less inclined to pay for exploited women; on the other hand, customers who think of prostitutes as objects and are more inclined to use women exploited by third parties (Anderson and O'Connell Davidson 2003: 25).

Yet who are these clients? And, more especially, who are the clients of cheap, rushed prostitution? The few investigations conducted until now show that nowhere do the men in question form a homogenous social group, either in their social-demographic characteristics, the kind of sexual services they demand or the ways in which they turn to prostitutes. The picture emerging from all the research in Europe suggests that a majority of more or less regular clients are middle-class men with a family and a stable position in society. According to recent studies, the percentage of clients in Europe's male adult population varies from 7 per cent in Britain to 39 per cent in Spain (Finland, 13 per cent; Norway, 11 per cent; Sweden, 13 per cent; the Netherlands, 14 per cent; Switzerland, 19 per cent; Russia, 10 per cent). In the United States, surveys show that 16 per cent of men have paid at least once for a sexual service, but that only 6 per cent do so on a regular basis (Hughes 2004: 10–11).

We know that the individuals in question often travel miles to get away from their neighbourhood or districts where they might be recognized; they seek nothing so much as anonymity (Censis 2002). In France most clients are men between 30 and 50 years of age, who live or have lived as part of a couple; 55 per cent of them have children (Bouamama 2004). In Italy there are thought to be at least 9 million more or less occasional customers of prostitutes, and 70 per cent of clients are married men. In Britain the typical client is a man aged about 30, married and quite well-off (Home Office 2004: 17). A study conducted in Stockholm in 2002 showed that at least 10 per cent of young men between 16 and 21 had been with a prostitute (Ministry of Industry, Employment and Communications of Sweden 2004). Of course, the data do not reflect the whole reality, but in Sweden too the typical client is a married man who has children and is living with a woman – or, often enough, a well-off man on a business trip. In any event, the research clearly indicates that most customers are well endowed with money, education and stability – the very things usually lacking for the women who prostitute themselves. Internationally, it seems that youth is one of the characteristics that customers seek in prostitutes: three-quarters express a preference for women below 25, and 22 per cent for girls aged 18 or less; only 6 per cent prefer women aged 30 or above (Anderson and O'Connell Davidson 2003: 19).

Although clients tend to be double the age of the women they meet, there is also quite a large component of young men. A comparative study of 175 clients from several countries (India, Italy, Thailand, Switzerland, Japan) found that approximately 78 per cent of respondents had first been with a prostitute when they were 21 or younger, and that approximately 18 per cent had been under 18 years of age (Anderson and O'Connell Davidson 2003: 18). In Europe it is quite common for small parties of students to use the search for a prostitute as a way of strengthening the group; they end an evening of drinking by heading for areas frequented by prostitutes. They might then spend two or three hours negotiating in the street or in nightspots, before they finally make their common choice of a woman.

Just as there is a wide spectrum of customers, so too do their guiding fantasies differ from one another. Surveys show that very often the sexual act itself is considered disappointing and is not the main concern of those who pay. The satisfaction may indeed be bound up much more with another part of the 'ritual': the preparations, the choice, or the reaching of an agreement. From a psychological point of view, recent research in France has identified four categories of motive leading clients to approach a prostitute. The first category, and the one most frequently encountered, consists of men who say they are emotionally alone and are using the cash nexus to find some relationship with the female sex. They justify their behaviour on the grounds that they are incapable of 'rising' to the level of a shared relationship with women. The second category consists of men who, because of failed relationships in the past, say they feel mistrust or a kind of fear towards the female sex; they try to find through prostitution a relationship of pure domination, in which the man is again the 'boss' and the woman a 'thing'. The third category turn to prostitutes to compensate for an unsatisfying sexual life in a couple; they draw a sharp distinction between their companion – worthy of respect and affection but uninterested in sex – and prostitutes wholly identified with the realm of the senses. The fourth and final category consists of men who, refusing commitment and responsibility, choose prostitution as an easy option that contains no hint of a future or a tie to another person (Bouamama 2004). In all four of these categories, relations with prostitutes are usually occasional, since, at least in the West, only a small share of the market consists of 'regulars' on terms of friendly familiarity with the women. There are also the very few who fall in love with a prostitute, or even marry one. On the other hand, if – to quote a 29-year-old Italian man – a prostitute 'decides to quit and change her life for a guy, once she decides on it she really takes it seriously, and the guy will then have by his side someone he can trust more than an office worker or an assistant in a chemist's shop' (Leonini 1999: 58).

The clients who populate the demand side are therefore very varied. We may conclude with two interesting quotations that show how prostitutes seem to perceive them:

There are all kinds of customer but the worst are certainly those who deny it and do not have the courage of their own action. The overwhelming majority play in life the part of honest men who nobody would blame for anything – crusading types, you know what I mean, who by day campaign against prostitutes and by night are the first to come looking for us. Then there are those who want to reopen the brothels, who would like the service to be guaranteed for themselves and their sons; those who never even ask what it means to buy a woman; those who know nothing about sex, neither the beautiful nor the ugly. (Corso and Landi 1998: 16–17)

Or again:

Clients are lumps of shit, that's all. Some can be decent and understanding, but it's best to say nothing about most of them! There are all kinds of customer, from the farmer to the engineer. They are people with problems.... They want to pour out the tensions and spite they feel towards someone, so they come and let it all out – far too much.... Then there are the more sensitive types, who are able to see why you're doing this work. (Corso and Landi 1998: 21)

The social role of the prostitute

What, if any, is the social function of prostitution? Since the nineteenth century, the main reading in Western theory has considered prostitution a 'necessary evil'. Georg Simmel, who argued this case most effectively at the start of the twentieth century, pointed out that prostitution had the precise social function of satisfying socially repressed male sexual needs which, if left unexpressed, would eventually be directed towards 'honest' virgins or married women.[1] The German philosopher–sociologist further thought that prostitution would retain this role of a 'necessary evil' so long as monogamous marriage continued to be the main institution regulating relations between men and women; it would become obsolete once such relations were based on free love, in a society where economic, social, intellectual and psychological opportunities for men and women were in harmony with each other.

With the perspective of a century, we can say that Simmel's predictions have not been fulfilled. The twentieth century saw a great liberalization of sexual mores in Western societies, but although the degree of sexual repression undoubtedly diminished the incidence of prostitution, it did not decline. Indeed, today it seems more widespread than in the years before 1968. The sexual liberalization is reflected more in the nature of the market, with a rise in transvestite and transsexual prostitution, and in payment for sex on the part of women (Weltzer-Lang, Barbosa and Mathieu, 1994). In contemporary societies, where greater equality between the sexes has been achieved and women are certainly more available for extramarital sexual encounters, it is no longer possible to consider prostitution a 'necessary evil'. Rather, it seems to be more and more strictly a 'consumption good'.

These shifts have occurred within a standardized cultural climate that has undergone profound changes since the late 1960s, and that appears to be more open to sexuality; both men and women, for example, display a growing interest in sexual activity unrelated to affect. Moreover, whereas strong censorship meant that until the 1960s there was no public dimension to the realm of sexuality, today the representation of sexual desire has a massive impact on everyday life through newspapers, television and the Internet. Images of naked women and, increasingly, of naked men, even gay men, in sexy poses, are used in publicity for all kinds of products; they have become an essential part of a culture that plays on sexual stimuli and, as Marcuse already noted, on the conversion of 'merchandise which has to be bought and used ... into objects of the libido' (Marcuse 1969: 12).

At the level of commercial sex proper, major cultural changes have also resulted from modernization and globalization of the market, which has made possible new models of consumption. New kinds of encounter between sellers and buyers – for example, through the Internet or so-called 'sex tourism' – have revolutionized the practices of prostitution, bringing together worlds that used to be far apart and enabling a 'standardization' of the market. Sex for payment also tends to derive legitimacy from the existence of a veritable industry that offers on a platter a range of ever more tempting services. Nor can there be any doubt that individuals, especially men, are solicited more than before to become consumers; new instruments such as the Internet and subscription television channels allow them to access services more discreetly and to refine and diversify their tastes. In general, neither the cultural nor the institutional context sets many limits to paid sex: the only restrictions are defined by purchasing power. The fact that, in the richer countries, women too are becoming interested in the purchase of sex is another sign of a market with libertarian and 'liberal' features.

Individuals seem more prepared to pay for sex then they were in the past, and their increased purchasing power certainly plays an essential role in the development of the market. As Ian Taylor and Ruth Jamieson (1999b) have shown, the rising consumption of sexual services can be understood only as part of wider cultural trends in market societies – that is, as part of the liberalization of trade and economic activity at a global level, and of the general re-organization of political and economic life around the sovereignty of citizen-consumers caught up in a whirlpool of consumerism. According to these two authors, the ceaseless quest to open up new markets, induced by the rise in purchasing power, has led to the colonization or commodification of sexuality itself. As we shall see, the search for commercial sex and the readiness to offer sex for payment tend to increase *pari passu* with the spread of the market economy on a world scale.

The mechanisms of this culture react in a one-to-one manner upon the dynamics underpinning the market: the same globally shared consumerist myths and mechanisms that lead clients to obtain sex on a monetary basis operate to make others prepared to enter the market as sellers of sexual services.[2] The pressure to regard the commodification of sex as an opportunity acts especially strongly on the minds of young women living in situations of great precariousness or hardship; this leads them to under-estimate the risks of exploitation that are often connected with the organization of such activity.

The exploitation of prostitution

Before we turn to a survey of the global sex market, it may be useful to set out a few problems. In the 1960s Marcuse analysed the growing commercialization of sex as evidence of what he called the 'repressive tolerance' of capitalist society, which created an island of 'sexual freedom' within a social landscape otherwise tightly controlled and regulated. In reality, as Taylor and Jamieson have argued (1999a), the potentially 'libertarian' features of the sex market – seen as a system counterposed to the repressive order – are themselves ever more clearly suppressed by the manner in which the market is organized. The prostitution market that revolves around sexual desire is based on a business structure of exploitation, and this means that, with rare exceptions, the only person to be 'liberated' is the one who pays, not the man or woman who prostitutes him- or herself. Internationalization of the market means that criminal networks living off the earnings of prostitution have spread in recent years and now constitute a major player. It is, of course, an aspect that tends to be hidden from view. Clients usually prefer to shut their eyes to it, for, as in any commercial transaction, they do not have to think about the other person from whom they are trying to get the most for the lowest possible price. Even if the mass media in nearly every country sound the alarm about extreme forms of exploitation (the so-called 'slave trade'), customers are frequently incapable of distinguishing between a victim of these forms and a woman who engages in prostitution on her own account. Or, in many cases, they pretend to be incapable of it. Since groups living off the earnings of prostitution camouflage themselves within a varied yet structured market, the client's position on the issue tends to remain ambivalent and unexpressed. The basic contradiction is clear enough: while it is true that in exceptional cases a client may help a woman to denounce her exploiters, it is also true that growing numbers of clients derive advantages from the system of exploitation, without which they would not have a constant fresh supply of pretty girls and young men willing to prostitute themselves for a small sum of money.

In short, clients prefer to maintain their traditional role, invisible, anonymous and free of responsibility.

Some factual evidence makes one wonder about this freedom from responsibility. For example, despite the high risk of infection with sexually transmitted diseases, clients still commonly request sex without a condom. Research in five regions of the United States has shown that nearly half the American and foreign clients of prostitutes claim to have unprotected sex, while 50 per cent of prostitutes of foreign origin and 73 per cent of Americans report that men pay more not to use a condom, and 29 per cent of the former and 45 per cent of the latter state that clients become aggressive when the woman insists on it (Gomez 2001: 11). In Europe, social workers stress that unprotected services are usually given by women trapped in the most brutal conditions of exploitation, who are forced to satisfy all their clients' demands or who themselves decide to keep some extra money for themselves by breaking the most elementary rules of hygiene and safety.

Data concerning the presence of under-age prostitutes in the adult market are hard to come by, but what we have show that it is a highly appreciated (and profitable) presence. According to UNICEF, 75 per cent of minors who prostitute themselves around the world do so within certain structures: hotels, brothels, nightclubs, restaurants. The figures, though hard to verify, are quite appalling: there are more than 200,000 exploited under-age prostitutes in the United States alone (Estes and Weiner 2001), and official reports from Europe that trafficking in (especially foreign) minors has recently intensified. In the Netherlands, Belgium, Italy and Germany, most of the recorded cases involve young people from Nigeria and Eastern Europe, especially Moldova. In Germany their presence is unmistakable among prostitutes subject to grave forms of exploitation, 90 per cent of whom come from countries to the east; in Western Europe as a whole, it is currently estimated that minors account for 10 to 30 per cent of this sector (Kelly 2002: 22), and in Russia and Eastern Europe they are thought to make up more than half the total. In Russian cities, both residents and passing customers make widespread use of under-age prostitutes: a study in 2000 in St Petersburg showed that more than 80 per cent of under-age prostitution involved girls and female children, 40 per cent of them aged under 14. Often they earn next to nothing for themselves, asking just what they need to buy food, drugs or a bottle of vodka (ECPAT 2003). The situation is also critical in south-east Europe, especially in Romania, a country of origin and transit towards Bosnia-Herzegovina, Albania, Kosovo and Italy. Here, 20 per cent of victims born in Romania or other East European countries are in the 13–15 age group, and another 33 per cent are between 15 and 20. Similarly, in Bulgaria, 30 per cent of young females who leave for foreign prostitution markets are under 18 (OSCE 2002).[3]

Finally, sociological research in various parts of the world has shown that clients often display contempt and racism in their dealings with foreign prostitutes; violent, or anyway disrespectful, behaviour appears to be widespread. Women from the Philippines or Russia who work as prostitutes in the United States say that customers do not see them as persons (Raymond 2002). In Europe the worst abuse seems to be reserved for African women, who often offer their services at knock-down prices: social workers trying to integrate them into the world of work observe a strong racial inferiority complex that is probably due to the mistreatment they have received. We may conclude from the little evidence at our disposal that, although the consumption of paid sex takes place within a new 'internationalized' framework of greater sexual freedom, it has retained many of its original characteristics. Above all, recourse to prostitution is still an almost exclusively male phenomenon and is felt as something to be kept secret: the individual client does not think his action immoral, but nor does he publicly admit to it. Society continues morally to disapprove of prostitution, and the figure of the prostitute is still strongly stigmatized.

Market trends

The global boom in commercial sex

The sex trade has considerably increased its turnover in the last decade. In Britain and elsewhere in Europe, there has certainly been a rise in the number of women, men, young people and transsexuals who prostitute themselves, most of them being women and girls.[4] It has been estimated that the commercial sex industry has a global turnover of $5,000 to $7,000 billion, greater than the combined military budget for the whole world (European Parliament 2004). The exceptional rate of growth in the sex market has been recorded not only in Europe but also in other 'developed' and 'underdeveloped' countries. Indeed one has the impression that in the 1980s and 1990s, in the world's main geographical concentrations of wealth, the more popular sectors of the market underwent huge expansion, until in many cases they reached true saturation point. Reliable figures are not available for America, partly because most of the individual states regard prostitution as an illegal activity, but we know that commercial sex is a profitable economic sector there and that, thanks to new technologies, the sex industry has become more diverse and sophisticated. The Internet has made it possible to advertise more secure contact systems: for example, porn videos transmitted by local cable channels may include a mention of websites through which it is possible to contact sellers of sexual services. The phenomenon has been spreading in Australia, where new laws have recently liberalized prostitution, while in Japan, where there was already massive growth in the

1980s, several tens of thousands of Filipino and Thai women alone are thought to be illegally employed in prostitution.

Another key region is the so-called 'transition countries' of East-Central Europe, the former Soviet Union and the Balkans. In this vast area the circuits of commercial sex, which until the late 1980s were quite small in scale, recorded a veritable boom in the course of the 1990s. The spread of prostitution has indeed been one of the most immediate effects of entry into the market economy. Straight after the collapse of the Communist regimes, which treated it as illegal, prostitution began to grow spontaneously through the initiative of individuals and small independent groups. It then became organized in a more thorough manner, until major business circuits took shape, partly connected with the global system through new technologies such as the Internet. One striking example of this is Hungary, where in the last decade prostitution has developed into a highly structured sex industry, alongside the production of pornographic videos and films. In the space of a few years the country has become one of the most thriving centres for commercial sex in Europe, and outstrips even Amsterdam or Copenhagen in the output of pornography. Other countries in East-Central Europe and the Balkans have registered similar rapid growth of sectors of the commercial sex market geared to the local population and foreign tourists, and at the same time a whole racket has specialized in the exploitation of prostitutes. According to one study conducted in 1997, the criminal organizations controlling the sector in Russia allow no autonomy to young women, who, in order to practise prostitution, have to hand over a large part of their earnings to groups of pimps well integrated into local mafia rackets (Caldwell, Galster and Steinzor 1997; IOM 2004b).

In the so-called 'developing' countries, women are often bought and sold and subjected to harsh exploitation within their own frontiers. Hundreds of thousands of women, driven to move from poverty-stricken regions to the urban centres, have supplied the raw material for the 'new' prostitution markets, not only in the former Soviet Union and the Balkans but also in Vietnam, Cambodia, China and all areas where the market economy has made giant strides in recent years. Sudden spurts in prostitution, mostly run by local racketeers, have also occurred in countries hit by war and the arrival of troops from abroad: Cambodia and Kosovo are just two well-known examples. Finally, the last decade has witnessed a sharp rise in (especially under-age) prostitution in African countries torn by war and political crises.

During the 1990s Southeast Asia consolidated its niche in the prostitution market, catering especially for international customers as a major source of invaluable foreign currency. In that part of the world, commercial sex is now one of the leading economic sectors, as we can see from an International Labour Office study carried out in Indochina, Indonesia, Thailand and Cambodia (Lin 1998). In Indonesia, annual income from this market is between $1.2 and $3.3 billion; and in Thailand it is between $22.5 and $27 billion, or 10–14 per cent of gross domestic product. Economists calculate that the sex business geared to foreigners and local customers has directly or indirectly contributed to the rise in employment and national income, as well as overall economic growth. It can turn over tens of billions of dollars, because it fits in with other expanding 'transnational' sectors such as the tourism and leisure industry and the whole travel market. Governments tacitly support such activity: they adopt on paper policies that criminalize prostitution, but these largely remain a dead letter.

Virtual travel and sexual desire

According to eminent scholars, the growing exploitation of women and children from the world's poorest countries is linked to the appalling amount of pornography on the web that shows young girls, boys and children, mostly of Asian, African, Latin American and Slav origin. On the web everything happens without regulation: the number of such pictures is enormous, and we do not know what techniques are used to convince those who make themselves available to pose and take part in sex shows. One major recent growth area has been the webcam business, which is based on the extreme exploitation of women in the Balkans (IOM 2004a). In general, over the last two decades, the sex industry has been recruiting more and more visibly in countries where low prices are paid for services. We know, for example, that in Europe actresses for the most dangerous or humiliating scenes in porn films come from countries in the east, where they are paid less than a third of the prices current elsewhere.[5]

Sex-related business on the Internet, partly based on forms of pimping, has increased at an astonishing rate (Council of Europe 2003); there are whole worlds out there, waiting to be discovered by anyone willing to pay to satisfy their sexual desires. The web offers the possibility of virtual (yet also effective) travel to infinite reality without even leaving home. Pages in a previously non-existent system of communication put customers almost directly in touch with people who prostitute themselves, and create almost unlimited scope for anyone with sufficient purchasing power. Stimuli of every kind pour forth from the web, and the supply of all manner of services and products seems to keep pace with the dizzying rise in demand. The various branches of the sex industry have thus become the trailblazer for major innovations: porn circuits were, for instance, the first to adopt credit-card transactions, multimedia content compression and marketing models that prefigured the use of video conferencing (Taylor and Jamieson 1999a). The results of this interdependence are plain to see: it has been estimated that, whereas in early 1995 there were some 200 websites selling erotic services and products (porn videos, contraceptives, sex toys, etc.), the number had risen to 28,000 by the end of 1997. In the United States pornographic material accounts for 60 per cent of all material sold on the web; in 1998 the turnover of this sector was approximately $1 billion, and at least three sites were each thought to have had a turnover of more than $100 million (Hughes 2000a). According to other studies, 70 per cent of the £252 million spent in Europe on the Internet went to pornographic sites (European Parliament 2004). Such success can be attributed mainly to psychological factors: the Internet ensures both privacy and rapid payment; it also allows people to follow their impulses in record time, so that a product can be sold before the customer has a chance to think twice about it.

Apart from the circulation of hard porn and the selling of services to individuals' homes, the Internet offers fast consultation of market guides to prostitution of all kinds and in every country; some websites gather detailed information about every corner of the world. The Internet has thus become the main place for the exchange of information among consumers: there are numerous sites where men swap and update reports, especially about the networks of so-called 'sex tourism', and this gives rise to a veritable culture of commodification of the female body. Special 'market products' seem to be emerging from the crystallization of stereotypes around certain physical and racial characteristics. African women and black women in general become objects of desire because of their supposedly 'savage' nature; Asian women because of their submissiveness and devotion; Latin Americans because of their capacity for passion; Europeans because of their lack of inhibitions; and young girls because of their freshness and docility. Some of the customers' reports dwell on the poverty and generally difficult situation of women in various countries, gleefully pointing to their total availability at bargain prices.

Travelling customers and the new horizons of paid sex

One peculiarity of the global prostitution market is that not only the sellers but also the buyers of sexual services move around in it. International tourism and business travel have turned prostitution into quite a rewarding business in many poor countries. Wherever it flourishes, and however it is run, prostitution for 'international' customers is tacitly accepted by governments, communities and families; often it is part of their strategy for survival.

In places where it forms part of the wider circuit of international tourism, prostitution is often one of the fastest expanding sectors of the economy, since demands and wishes of the travellers have a great influence over the structure of supply in local societies (Leheny 1995). The prostitution circuits provide income to those who organize them, as well as attracting investment and expanding the circulation of money. Although the geography of commercial sex is already highly structured, new areas emerge every year and create new specializations. Africa is beginning to exercise a strong attraction for Western women: in Gambia, for instance, female tourism in search of (sometimes under-age) boys, known as 'bombstars' or 'beachboys', is a growing phenomenon, and female sex tourism is also widespread in Jamaica, on the Caribbean coasts and in Goa (O'Connell Davidson 1998: 180–83). But it is above all for male pleasure-seekers on vacation that the submissive, compliant and exotic image of overseas women holds an irresistible fascination. Asian and Latin women, in particular, are marketed as sexually tireless and uninhibited, with the qualities necessary to satisfy customers in full. Brazil continues to have a lot of success, being a country where attractive women abound and the prostitution market includes at least half a million minors, but the Dominican Republic, Colombia, Cuba and some of the English-speaking Caribbean islands are other well-known centres in the Americas. Highly organized prostitution markets also exist in Panama, Surinam and Curaçao, where women and young girls receive a tiny fraction of their earnings and make themselves available to clients for days or weeks at a time.[6] Moreover, alongside this sector based on intensive exploitation, there is usually a do-it-yourself prostitution that satisfies the persistent demand from foreign tourists through the more informal channels supplied by taxi drivers, hotels or the street.

In Southeast Asia, the world 'leader' in commercial sex, circuits for international customers have not developed spontaneously, as a 'natural' response to the appearance of tourist money, but have followed in the wake of wars or other traumatic events. In Thailand, for instance, prostitution suddenly took on outlandish proportions in the 1970s to satisfy the demand from American troops serving in Vietnam (Stienstra 1996), who could choose to spend Rest & Recreation periods there soaking up drugs and paid sex. When the troops returned to the United States, the Thai brothel-owners – who by then formed a wealthy elite – decided to reorient their business to local men, German and Japanese businessmen, and tourists. The government tacitly supported this initiative. Holidays including sex tours went on sale especially in Japan, where they also became immediately popular as company perks, but then the new package trips began to be marketed to an ever wider public. The sales pitch was so successful that prostitution developed into one of the country's main international attractions. From the mid-1990s on, the Internet made it possible to expand the space for publicity on a global scale, so that a major new impetus was given to the sector. Korean, Malaysian and Chinese men have become regular clients of Thai brothels, and Asian elites in general, beginning to feel their way in the market economy, often combine pleasure with their business trips.[7]

When the sex business was taking off in Thailand, the circuits did not include Vietnam, Laos and Cambodia, where successive armed conflicts had been taking place and prostitution was forbidden. In Cambodia, the arrival in 1991 of 100,000 UN peacekeeping troops and officials was the main impetus for an unprecedented growth of prostitution, and the trafficking of girls and women from rural areas to the city became the source of highly valued foreign currency. By 1993, when the troops began to withdraw, it was estimated that at least 20,000 women and girls were selling themselves for sex, and the subsequent development of the market economy has further expanded the sector and oriented it to local customers. In 1996, according to some estimates, 57,000 women were being exploited in these circuits, 70 per cent of them in the two main cities: Phnom Penh and Battambang (Hughes 2000a). Over time the average age has decreased: child prostitution is very profitable for brothel-owners, who are thought locally to make $3,000 or more from each girl. Today a third of all prostitutes in Cambodia – at least 16,000 individuals – are minors, many of them of Vietnamese origin. The market economy has also given a spur to prostitution (including child prostitution) inside Vietnam itself. The migration flows feeding the market consist mainly of young Chinese peasant girls, sold by their impoverished families for a handful of dollars and forced to work in conditions of semi-slavery.

The situation is different in the Philippines, a country which for many decades has been intensively exporting women for exploitation in the United States. The sex market inside the country, including minors, sprang up around the US naval bases to satisfy the demand of the large number of men serving there. The same areas then gradually became a destination for sex tourists, so that today it is estimated, for example, that each year at least 13,000 Australians visit Angeles City, a well-known district close to a large American military camp. According to local studies, the foreign clients have an average age of 30–35 and are in large part professionals such as judges, lawyers and teachers. Social workers report that men who arrive on sex tours can rarely distinguish between adult women and minors (Sturdevant Pollock and Stoltzfus 1992) – a highly convenient confusion, because it frees them of any sense of guilt and enables them to abuse the very young with impunity.

In general, paid sex has become a more or less visible component of mass tourism: escape to faraway lands increasingly involves not only a quest for exotic flavours, scents and panoramas but also experience of local eroticism as the best route to 'complete well-being'. Everything comes at a price, of course. When the tourist-client is on holiday, away from his usual environment, he feels free to indulge desires to which he would otherwise never admit; the limitations of his usual identity go by the board, since now none of his close circle can see and recognize him. He thinks of the destination as a 'heaven on earth' where the normal moral constraints – which forbid him to pay for sex with a 14-year-old girl – no longer have any meaning. He tends to find suitable justification for such behaviour: for example, he convinces himself that in this country prostitution is not a sin and sexual abuse is considered normal, or (as we learn from interviews in Southeast Asia) that young girls are by nature sharper and inclined to humour men from a tender age, or that they have no problems working as prostitutes and are actually quite lucky to be doing so, since they earn more than others of their age and are able to meet interesting people (O'Connell Davidson 1998; Seabrook 1996).

Davidson and Taylor have identified three categories of British sex tourists in Pattaya, Thailand: (1) 'macho lads', who travel in groups and see the place as one big amusement park where they can scooter around, visit clubs, get good sex, play pool and watch live sex shows; (2) 'Mr Average', an older married or divorced man, who travels alone on a package trip looking for pseudo-emotional, pseudo-romantic adventures; and (3) 'cosmopolitan men', leisure or business travellers, who deny being sex tourists but happily take advantage of the services made available to them (1994: 2–3). In each case, the tourist does not want to look beyond appearances or to notice the harsh school that young girls are put through to make them compliant. Wherever sex tourism spreads, the exploitation of minors tends to grow exponentially: not only young boys but above all young girls, who are highly appreciated by consumers of paid sex. As we have seen, foreign clients take cover behind the difficulty of guessing the age of a girl from a different ethnic group, and – even if we exclude the paedophile sector, which is organized in different ways – the percentage of minors in these markets is very high. The situation is deeply disturbing: the main international effort is still at the state of creating systems for the protection of minors, and in December 2001 the second World Congress against Commercial Sexual Exploitation of Children, held in Yokohama, Japan, paid great attention to the issue of sex tourism.[8]

Migrant prostitutes and the transnational market

Pretty, exotic and cheap

Although the forms of organization and contract vary from place to place,[9] all the sex markets that have recently undergone expansion have two common features: the development of low-price sectors into a mass phenomenon, and an accentuation of their trans-national character. In fact, these two features are closely linked. Whether in Denmark or Thailand, Britain or Japan, recent young immigrants have become highly competitive within the local prostitution scene. This is because, as in other areas of economic activity, immigrants have to work longer hours for less pay, and with less attention to their own safety. This tendency appears everywhere. In Poland today the most exploited prostitutes are of Bulgarian or Roma origin; in India they are young girls from Bangladesh and Nepal; in Cambodia they are mostly Vietnamese, in Vietnam Chinese, and in South Africa Mozambican.

In the countries of Western Europe, a catchment basin for migration from every corner of the world, the lowest rates are charged by 'non-EU' women, especially those from Africa, Eastern Europe and the Balkans. Their constant flow into the cheapest sectors of the sex market has led to an improvement in the quality of services on offer and, at the same time, to a fall in prices. The benefits for customers are obvious, since the women and girls are younger, more attractive and more available, while the prices of their services are lower. It is a surprising but little noted fact that prices in the cheaper sectors have not changed for more than a decade. In London, as officers in the Charing Cross police district point out, the price for sex services is not even one pound higher than fifteen years ago, whereas over the same period rental costs, for example, have increased threefold. The police are of the view that the number of women, all intensely competing with one another, must have doubled or tripled (Shelley 2000). Nor is the phenomenon limited to London. In the United States, the price for the sexual services of an under-age Mexican girl hovers around $25. On the streets of Italy and France, a customer pays an average of €20–30 for penetrative sex with a condom – the same as what a drug addict engaged in occasional street prostitution could charge twenty years ago.

The competition is intense, now that half the women prostituting themselves in Europe are immigrants. They started to become a major presence in the late 1980s, and today foreign women play an essential role in the markets of every country: from a minimum of 30 per cent in Ireland (where the sex sector is less important) to 65 per cent in the Netherlands (where the sex business is highly structured). In Germany foreign women are thought to make up 50 per cent of the market, with a total of 150,000, while in Denmark (where there are more than one hundred Thai massage parlours) they account for 35 per cent. The corresponding figure for Finland is 40 per cent, and for France 60 per cent (Lehti 2003).

In all the countries of Western Europe, in varying proportions, women arrive from distant areas such as Latin America and the Caribbean, southern and sub-Saharan Africa and the Far East, and a growing number from Central Europe, the Baltic states, the Balkans and the former Soviet Union. The majority of women and girls come from Albania, Lithuania, Moldova, Romania, Russia and Ukraine. As in the case of the United States, other places of origin are Southeast Asia (especially Thailand) and Latin America (especially Mexico, Colombia, Brazil and the Dominican Republic), with North and West Africa (especially Morocco and Nigeria) also substantively represented (Lehti 2003). It is a truly multiethnic market. It has been estimated that today 90 per cent of the 6,000 prostitutes in Vienna are immigrants; whereas in the 1980s a majority of new arrivals were from Asia, in the 1990s there was a sizeable influx from Latin America, especially the Dominican Republic, and from Eastern Europe. As for London, the Metropolitan Police reckon that 70 per cent of women working as prostitutes in bars and clubs are of foreign origin (Home Office 2004: 75), and elsewhere in Britain thousands of foreign women have been brought in to work in apartments, saunas and massage parlours. Antislavery International indicates a highly diverse origin, with hundreds of women trafficked each year from Albania, Lithuania, Russia, Ukraine and Romania, as well as Nigeria, China and Sierra Leone. It is estimated that, of the

80,000 people who prostitute themselves, at least a quarter come from the Balkans, the former Soviet republics and Thailand (Lehti 2003). Some research suggests that a majority of the girls working in British brothels and massage parlours are of Albanian or Thai origin (Protection Project 2002b: 536), and one Home Office study reports that these women are often ruthlessly exploited by local traffickers and criminal gangs (Kelly and Regan 2000). The aspect that seems to worry the British authorities most is the widespread exploitation, not only in the major cities but also in provincial towns where one would not expect there to be a large presence of foreign prostitutes. In Spain too, where similar forms of exploitation have been recorded, most of the women come from Spanish-speaking countries (especially the Dominican Republic and Colombia) and Africa. In the Netherlands, on the other hand, there is a large presence of young people from East-Central Europe and Africa (especially Nigeria), and the flows have been increasing from the former Yugoslavia, Hungary and the Baltic states. In France, a majority of new arrivals are from Albania, Kosovo, the Czech Republic, Slovakia, Lithuania, Romania and Bulgaria, with a considerable number from Latin America and Africa (Lehti 2003). According to the US State Department, women working as prostitutes in the United States – especially in California, Florida, New York, Hawaii, Georgia, Alaska, Texas and North Carolina – tend to come mainly from distant lands in Asia (Thailand, the Philippines, South Korea, China), Eastern Europe and the former Soviet Union. Large numbers also originate in Mexico, the Caribbean and Central America (especially Jamaica, Honduras and Guatemala (Mattar 2004)), while in Canada the main flows are from Southeast Asia, the former Soviet Union and the Balkans (OSCE 2002).

The movements from these areas tend to alternate, in accordance with certain broad lines and dynamics that we shall try to illustrate below. In each country, young women with various origins succeed one another in occupying particular areas and sectors of the market. The arrival of a new intake sets in motion powerful mobility mechanisms, as rackets and activity patterns weakened by the police forces are gradually replaced by fresher circuits that exploit younger people with less experience. Women entering the prostitution market for the first time lack expertise and can easily be subjected to serious exploitation and rapid transfer. For that reason a kind of diversification operates in the sex market. On the one hand, there is a growing specialization and 'professionalization' of women in upmarket sectors, consisting mainly of locals but also of foreigners well integrated into the social life of the host country. On the other hand, there is exponential growth in the number of women working for cheap rates in mass sectors of the market, mostly newcomers not integrated into the host country and nearly always lacking residence permits. These women tend to live in a state of perpetual motion: as we shall see, both in Europe and Japan, the United States and Russia, the organization of their activity may involve constant movement between various towns and countries.

Of course, the arrival of young and cheap immigrant prostitutes capable of enduring major risks and suffering has fuelled the more popular sector of the market, changing its features and gradually creating new hierarchies. But it would be misleading to explain the phenomenon in terms of two different types of prostitution: one mainly practised by women born in the country, and another, more 'popular' sector, mostly worked by foreigners. The scenarios of arrival are many and complex, and the market position occupied by immigrant prostitutes is itself quite varied. Clients do not think of them as a single group but divide them into various subgroups corresponding to a precise ethnic or racial classification. In all countries, clients identify certain groups, or certain bars and clubs, as the lowest link in the chain and look for more desirable sex workers instead – a grading system in which white European women very often occupy the highest positions (Anderson and O'Connell Davidson 2003: 21–3). It should also be mentioned that, in some contexts with a strong ethnic mix, prostitution circuits have taken shape for clients of a particular ethnicity: many places in New York's Chinatown, for example, make prostitutes available only to Chinese customers. In some cases the restrictions have a regional character, so that access to the place of prostitution is open only to people speaking a certain dialect: for example, those who present various linguistic peculiarities in certain places in Mexico (Gomez 2001: 69). Similarly, in Australia many Asian premises are frequented only by Vietnamese and Chinese customers. Nevertheless, these remain exceptions to the rule, and most foreign women work in the market intended for men originating in the country in question.

Living and working conditions

In general, foreign women who sell sexual services – so-called 'sex workers' – may receive very high remuneration or, on the contrary, be incredibly badly paid. The widely ranging treatment depends both on the circuit in which the activity is carried out and on the way in which it is organized. The circuits may be visible (as in street prostitution) or invisible, legal or illegal. One of the forms of hidden prostitution involves call girls who operate from an apartment, or women who approach clients in night clubs, bars or restaurants. Some girls work in saunas, massage parlours, beauty parlours and sex clubs; others make themselves available for hotel customers; still others make home visits after being chosen on the Internet or at an agency. There are ballet dancers and escort girls who prostitute themselves from time to time, with a few select clients; and there are women who hang around in partner-swapping clubs. The varied world of prostitution is largely invisible to those who do not frequent it, but this does mean that it is not significant. Whereas in Italy the hidden sector occupies a little more than half the market, in many other countries, such as Germany, Austria or the United States, it accounts for nearly all of it.

The percentage of foreign women varies, as does their market position. Even if they are not all victims of serious exploitation, they tend to be more vulnerable all over the world. A comparative study based on interviews with American women and Russian or other ex-Soviet women who prostitute themselves in the United States has identified important differences in their work rhythms – although there are also exceptions to this general rule. The Russian women say they serve anywhere between 3 and 30 clients a day, while the locally born women have an average of 3–7 clients a day, and only habitual drug-users increase this number to 20 or even 30. There also seem to be differences in the type of services they give: whereas a third of the Russian women say their clients sometimes request deeply humiliating services, the American women report more normal demands such as oral or vaginal sex (Raymond 2002).

To explain these differences, it is useful to establish a kind of 'exploitation scale' in the world of prostitution. At one extreme is the sector of independent prostitution, where women have considerable freedom to bargain with clients and keep all their earnings for themselves; at the other extreme is the world of trafficking and enslavement, where women have no say over their forms or rhythms of work and little capacity to negotiate with clients, and where they keep none but the barest pittance from their earnings. In the middle, work scenarios involve agreements with various kinds of arrangers, and are based on various degrees of consent and subordination. Relations between women and arrangers may be consensual and sometimes even come close to independent prostitution, but they may also involve relations of subjugation that result in exploitation properly so called. Immigrant women can be found at every point in this scale, but the disadvantages bound up with their legal position and lack of integration into society mean that they usually find it more difficult to reach the level of an independent prostitute. Even in the best of cases, they have to face higher start-up costs and greater logistical difficulties: they must pay for their own travel and find a protected set-up in a new environment; they often do not speak the local language and, not having contacts of their own, have to trust middlemen to find customers for them.

One thing should be made clear here. The estrangement effect that follows the immigrant's 'social uprooting' is certainly more extreme in the case of women who prostitute themselves for the first time in a foreign country. According to social workers, once these girls and young women emigrate and are more or less forced into prostitution, their perception of the world changes inexorably; only a major personality change can enable them to face this kind of life. If they are not to go under in their daily encounters with pimps, younger rivals and customers, they must quickly learn to use coarse and aggressive forms of behaviour – and to rely on themselves alone. Their life develops at best within the micro-community of women in a similar situation to their own: their daily existence, as social workers have noted, is dominated by difficult workplaces, often decrepit, costly and overcrowded, where the group keeps constant watch on them. At least in the early months they are often unable to communicate with the outside world except in the few words indispensable for negotiations with customers. The new food they have to eat is often poor in quality and unbalanced, the rhythms of sleeping and waking are completely unnatural, and the conditions of cultural isolation prove hard to endure. Finally, for young women who come from countries with a very different culture and mentality, the fact that they are newcomers as well as new at their job often puts them in a weak bargaining position with clients. The youngest seem to be the least adroit in this respect, as they are constantly switched from place to place in order to be 'new to the market'; these are the girls in direst need who, as we have seen, do not baulk at many unprotected 'special services' to get the better of the competition. Many of them do not correspond to the still current stereotype of the coarse and gaudy prostitute, even if their experience of prostitution is very harsh – especially as many clients express a perverse sexuality that they find hard to accept. Physical violence and theft are common occurrences, even at the hands of the police, and there is a tendency for them to overcome stress and tiredness by abusing drugs and alcohol. Hard drugs have also been widely administered in Europe in recent years to make women more docile, and to tie them more strongly to their pimps. Sometimes the girls are also used as drug pushers (Lehti 2003). In the United States the trend seems to have stabilized at a point where the great majority of prostitutes, both foreign (87 per cent) and indigenous (92 per cent), regularly take drugs or alcohol to perform their duties (Gomez 2001: 12).

Independent prostitutes, exploited women and victims of trafficking

If we look at the prostitution market as a whole, keeping in mind the viewpoint and motivation of those who enter it to work, we may identify four different types (Phongpaichit, Piriyarangsan and Treerat 1998: 197–205). The first consists of attractive, enterprising women who engage in well-paid ongoing activity from a position of independence and seek to minimize the risks of the trade. Many of these first went into prostitution because of the high earnings it offered, and some think of it as a job like any other from which they can make a good living. The second type consists of women who prostitute themselves on an occasional basis, also from a position of independence; their motives may be similar to those of the first group. The third type, however, consists of women who have been driven to prostitution by grave economic pressures and a lack of other opportunities; they enter it in a subordinate position and often have to submit to extreme forms of exploitation. The fourth and last type consists of victims of trafficking, women who have been forced or blackmailed into prostitution in various ways, and cheated about the nature or the conditions of the work. The four worlds sometimes connect with one another, and individuals may sometimes move between them. One woman may manage to escape the mechanisms of trafficking and become more or less independent, while another may fall into the debt trap and be handed over, or sold, to other pimps, who then reduce her to slavery and pocket the full proceeds of her activity.

The sexual services of foreign women are offered on the market at various prices and in a number of different forms. As we have already stressed, women from one particular ethnic group – which varies from country to country – sometimes occupy the most desirable positions in the market, while women from other ethnic groups occupy the least advantageous niches. The way in which their work is organized does indeed vary a great deal. Foreign women belonging to the first group, who prostitute themselves on an independent basis, are usually individuals with a background of similar activity in their country of origin; they have used good contacts to obtain a proper residence permit, or even full citizenship, perhaps by means of a marriage of convenience. For only those whose papers are in order can strike out on their own and join native-born professionals on an equal footing (Carchedi et al. 2000).

Our second type, the occasional prostitutes, are mainly women who are driven to supplement their own income through prostitution, usually without being sucked into the ongoing mechanisms of exploitation. Many are young women who work as strippers or as extras in porn videos, trying to find a way into an artistic career and making occasional use of prostitution. For them, too, it is sometimes necessary to come to terms with those who run the prostitution market, especially with the owners of clubs or agencies or men who control a streetwalker's patch. In Italy, for example, a woman must often pay €30 to €50 a day in protection money to a criminal gang that runs the street where she intends to work (Europap/Tampep 2001).

The third group, subject to ongoing forms of exploitation, mainly comprises young immigrants from economically backward areas of Eastern Europe, the Balkans, Africa and Southeast Asia. In the United States they often come from Mexico. A woman who engages in this kind of prostitution, on the street or in closed premises such as an apartment or a hotel, is flanked by people who claim a high percentage of her earnings. The part of the market that involves the use of violent methods and extreme forms of exploitation varies in size according to place and circumstances, and it is always hard to tell what proportion of the total market it constitutes. In France it seems to be large: an OSCE report estimates that 80 per cent of prostitutes in the big cities are subject to some degree of severe exploitation (OSCE 2002). The proportion is considerable elsewhere in Europe too. In London, prostitutes working in special premises usually have to hand over half their earnings to the person running them. But they do have freedom of movement, live independently in flats or small hotels and are entitled to days off: in short, they have some social and personal life of their own. However, studies have shown that even the more contractual and protected work relations involve an obligation that leaves little space for private life. Thai women working in Copenhagen massage parlours, for example, spend nearly all their time on the premises, which are open twenty-four hours a day; their arrangement with the owner (often a Thai woman with a Danish husband) means that they usually hand over 40 per cent of their earnings and keep the other 60 per cent. The three to five girls in each establishment often spend the day in rooms measuring 10–12 square metres, eating, drinking and watching television while they wait for the next customer. They receive an average of 3–9 customers a day, and their earnings vary greatly from place to place. Interviews show that these women are not really integrated into the life of the city: even if they have permission to go out, they rarely have occasion to do so. Their contacts are usually limited to their husband (if they are married), the customers and a few people connected with the work. They have no trust in the public authorities and rely on informal networks even to borrow money (on usurious terms). Some of what they earn is wasted on gambling or luxury goods: 'easy come, easy go', as they put it. But the respondents manage to send an average of 60–80 per cent of their income back to their home country, where it is used to build modern housing. 'Typically the women invest a lot of time and money trying to keep in contact with their families back home. In this way they struggle to maintain their influence and position as mothers, wives or daughters. But a lot of them clearly suffer from homesickness and frustration' (Lisborg 2002: 110). They present high levels of psychological depression, which stems from the feeling that they are 'polluted' and socially stigmatized. Yet, although the work is hard to endure, the relatively high earnings make it difficult for them to give it up.

The fourth category, the victims of trafficking at the bottom of the scale, are usually women who have been forced into prostitution in the face of threats to kill them or their family. Their exploiters pocket all, or nearly all, their earnings. They are therefore unable to achieve the dream of making enough money to change their life, either when they return home or here and now in the host country. Trafficking involves a special relationship of exploitation, the harshest kind, which mainly affects foreign women unable to defend themselves. The treatment to which they are subjected differs considerably from that of other prostitutes. In Britain, for example, where earnings in brothel-like establishments are usually divided fifty–fifty between the woman and the organizer, victims of trafficking receive next to nothing yet have to put up with a larger number of clients and to perform more expensive services (Kelly and Regan 2000: 26). In Greece, according to one study, pimps earn eight to ten times more from a victim of trafficking than from a woman who has grown up in the country (Kelly 2002: 44). Evidence from the countries of origin confirms this picture: the International Organization for Migration (IOM), for example, estimates that women from the Kirghiz republic exploited in Russia and Europe manage to keep an average of 3–5 per cent of their earnings. Sometimes they may receive a fixed sum for their services. A 30-year-old Romanian woman, for example, divorced with children, was exploited by an Albanian clan in Italy and received the equivalent of €250 a month:

> The money was transferred by a bank to Romania. I never knew who paid it to me. If I hadn't accepted these conditions, I don't dare think what would have happened, given the constant threats and pressures I was subjected to. (Tribunale di Lecce 2000e)

In some cases, the payment is set at €5–7 for a day's work. In Kosovo in 2003, in brothels where clients paid €100–150 an hour, the women said that they received €100–130 a month and regularly sent it back home. This was a significant sum and provided a strong incentive for them to remain there (IOM 2004a: 58). In Japan an exploited Filipino woman might make $233 a month, in clubs where an hour with a prostitute costs the customer around $310, although it is possible that earnings might rise as high as $465 to $1,550 a month (Leones and Caparas 2002). In Israel, pimps charge an average of 100–600 shekels for each service, while the women receive 20 shekels – and even that only once they have repaid the debt for their travel and keep (Levenkron and Dahan 2003). In such cases, what should be a clear distinction between exploitation and trafficking seems to have disappeared. It is true that the women have an economic interest in remaining, since the sums they make appear huge when converted into their own currency and could never be earned back home. But it is equally clear that they are subjected to extremes of exploitation and trapped within the mechanisms of the sex trade.

To recognize a victim of trafficking, we must keep in mind not so much any earnings she may make as the kind of life she is forced to lead. NGO reports in all parts of the world describe victims of trafficking as women and girls who live in conditions of semi-imprisonment: the only people with whom they have dealings are pimps, clients, the police and fellow prostitutes. Compelled to operate in brothels or on the street, they endure the harshest forms of harassment as well as constant mental and physical violence. Blackmail usually prevents them from reporting their own exploitation, and only in fortunate cases are they in a position to meet social workers or doctors. The criminal gangs, who are quite capable of threatening the women and even killing them, engage in fairly uniform kinds of exploitation. Their victims from all over the world, whether working on the street or in brothels, speak of similar kinds of treatment, forced to work as much as ten or fifteen hours for days at a time, and sometimes kept under round-the-clock observation. Time off is at the boss's discretion and may be limited to the first few days of the menstrual cycle, although sometimes the women may be forced to perform oral sex during this period. In many cases, girls are simply refused permission to go out during their free time. The techniques are similar from the United Arab Emirates through Japan and Spain to the United States. In Florida, for example, the Chain Group rotated Mexican girls among a number of brothels, subjecting 14-year-olds to feverish rates of work, with as many as 130 clients a week. They received $3 for each service and were kept hostage through blackmail and physical and mental violence. Everything spent on their daily living was magnified and added to their debt of two or three thousand dollars; it was obviously very difficult to clear this debt, which included the cost of everything, sometimes even an abortion (Protection Project 2000). In a context of trafficking, what the clients pay always goes directly to the exploiters, but the same exploiters charge the women for board and lodging, condoms, clothing, make-up and even petrol for the driver accompanying them, or bus tickets to reach their place of work. Debt is the key means of subjugation, and the women are forced to live under varying degrees of intensive supervision.

The actual form of confinement varies with the type of organization: in India, as in Germany or Poland, women are held in clandestine brothels, where the windows are often barred; elsewhere those who work the streets are controlled through mobile phones. More 'homespun' forms of exploitation, by individual pimps or small groups, usually involve living with a pimp and maintaining an often dubious relationship with him, so that a woman's blackmailer may also sleep beside her every night and demand unprotected sexual relations, resulting in unwanted pregnancies and abortions. Apart from working as a prostitute, she will have to take care of the flat where they live, prepare meals, clean the place and look after her exploiters. There are also a lot of women in the field, who run every aspect of the girls' lives and demand total obedience from them by threatening repercussions for their family back home.

The broad outlines of the system are always the same. At first, the woman earns nothing at all for herself, because she has to reimburse everything that the traffickers spent on her journey and installation in the new locality. After a few months, the girl can begin to send home a modest sum and keep enough for an occasional meal out (although usually she will make do with a sandwich while waiting between clients), as well as for a few luxuries and beauty products. Different methods are used to make her sustain the rhythm of work: African girls, for example, are often forced to pay a fine if they earn less than the norm in any one day, while pimps in the Balkans prefer to beat up girls who do not make enough. If, as the months pass, the woman gradually manages to earn well and to gain the trust of her exploiters, she will be able to negotiate better treatment; the maximum she can achieve is an agreement that allows her to keep up to 50 per cent of what she earns. Such concessions, obtained only after persistent demands, often come at a high price, since the woman in question is forced to add hours that she organizes herself to the peak hours of the day when her earnings go to the group of exploiters. Her workload may therefore increase enormously. Another method in use from Israel to Japan to Croatia is to report women for residence permit irregularities once they have paid off their debt. In this way, the gangs eliminate competition and keep a free hand to exploit new women through the techniques of trafficking.

Clients should know that, for a woman controlled by a criminal racket who makes as much as €10,000 to €15,000 a month, the earning of money is mostly only an objective for the long term, or a mirage. The mirage does have great importance, however. After all the physical violence and psychological traumas, the prospect of achieving at least one basic goal of her migration – earning money – may provide a strong incentive to keep going and put up with the worst humiliations. For it is very difficult to return home when the only thing to show for the trip is an extra burden of sorrows. The woman therefore tries to hold out and, if possible, to change the situation slowly to her advantage. The continual passage of money through her hands encourages her to be patient, in the belief that one day some of it can be hers and make her situation radically different. The ties of dependence that her male or female exploiters establish with her also play on such mechanisms. For the woman remains entangled in a relationship of subjugation, although over time she tries to win greater margins of autonomy and a larger share of her earnings. As Kathleen Barry has shown (1979), the relationship is similar to that between a master and a slave: the exploiter must gain control over the woman's mind, so that she is not only obedient but loyal and capable of self-discipline. The techniques we have been discussing usually mean that he is successful.

Trafficking as an international problem

What is trafficking, exactly? Wijers and Lap-Chew draw a distinction between two stages in the trafficking in women (recruitment and exploitation) but identify coercion as a fundamental element in both. Trafficking is thus defined as any activity related to the recruitment and/or transport of a person within or beyond the national frontiers, whose end goal is to extract labour or services with the use or threat of violence, abuse of authority or a position of domination, trickery, the manipulation of debt, or other

violent means (Wijers and Lap-Chew 1997: 36). Forced labour
and/or slavery-like practices occur when the labour or services of
a woman are obtained by appropriating her legal identity and/or
physical person, through deception, the debt system or other
violent means (Wijers and Lap-Chew 1997: 36).[10] However, the
most widely shared international definition of human trafficking
is the one given in 2000 in the framework of the United Nations
Convention against Transnational Organized Crime, known as
the Palermo Convention (2000).[11] This definition, which does not
place much stress on the phase of exploitation, is very important
because it laid the basis for a shared international usage and sig-
nalled a gradual homogenization of policies to combat trafficking. But, despite these recent advances, there is still no standard
international way of assessing the scale of the phenomenon. The
US State Department estimates that 800,000 to 900,000 persons
are trafficked each year throughout the world, while other US
official agencies consider that each year 600,000 to 800,000 persons (70 per cent female, and 50 per cent under age) fall victim
to international recruitment, transport and exploitation, at least
half of them for the purposes of sexual exploitation. Furthermore,
between 2 and 4 million persons are purportedly subject to human
trafficking within their national frontiers (US Department of State
2004). Estimates of the total size of the business vary widely: some
calculations suggest that the trafficking of young women and girls
as semi-slaves for the global sex market has an annual turnover
of at least $7 billion (Lehti 2003: 51); and, if this is set beside the
$52 billion figure for the sex industry as a whole (Hughes 2000a),
we can see that the sector based on methods of extreme violence
represents a large share of the market. It should be said that these
totals are not very reliable, one of the main difficulties being that
sexual exploitation often takes place in places that are neither
monitored nor even visible to the outside eye.

Although much attention has been given in recent years to the issue of human trafficking, not even rough estimates have yet been made of the proportion of trafficking victims in the total number of prostitutes; nor have there been special studies to calculate what percentage of women working as prostitutes are subject to forms of exploitation. The gravity of the phenomenon is beyond doubt, however, and alarming figures have been released in more assiduous countries such as the Netherlands. The Dutch police claim that only the tip of the iceberg is visible, since most of the women in question do not report abuse for fear of the repercussions, but they think that at least 750 trafficking organizations operate in the country and that nearly 90 per cent of female prostitutes from East-Central Europe are brought there by traffickers. The Task Force on Trafficking, part of the Organization for Security and Cooperation in Europe (OSCE), estimates that there are 4,000 victims of trafficking in Vienna (US Department of State 2004: 210). In Britain the figure is reportedly between 142 and 1,420 per annum, but some experts would put it much higher (Kelly, Regan 2002: 22; UK Government 2004). The authorities themselves consider it difficult to measure the scale of the phenomenon: the Metropolitan Police, for example, does no more than vaguely state that a majority of women working in brothels are foreigners, that a high proportion of them are illegal immigrants, and that some of these are victims of trafficking (UK Government 2004). Nevertheless, special police squads active in the last couple of years have identified more than five hundred foreign women working as prostitutes in Soho, in central London, and suggest that there has been a 20 per cent rise over the past five years. It should also be stressed that whereas in 1995 Balkan women were almost non-existent in the area, they now make up some 80 per cent of the total; and that a majority of these have been trafficked (Kelly 2002: 11). In the case of Italy, the IOM puts the number of foreign female victims of trafficking at between 20,000 and 30,000, while the turnover from their prostitution is thought to amount to some €90 million a year. Statistics are more forthcoming in countries where prostitution is more visible, and so it is no accident that the most detailed figures in Europe apply to Italy, where the number of brothels is increasing but until recently 50 per cent of prostitution took place on the streets. In general, the partial collection of international statistics does allow us to identify some of the main routes. According to the UN Office on Drugs and Crime, the countries mentioned in various reports throughout the world as places of origin are, in descending order of frequency, Ukraine, Russia, Nigeria, Albania, Moldova and Bulgaria, followed by China, Thailand, the Czech Republic, Lithuania and Poland (Kangaspunta 2003: 95–6); the transit countries most often mentioned are all in East-Central Europe. As to the destination countries, the ones most often cited are Italy, the United States and Germany (Kangaspunta 2003: 95–6). All the main routes are from countries with a strong patriarchal culture, or ones where the political and economic position of women has recently deteriorated, to countries with greater gender equality, as well as from poorer to richer parts of the world.

The international debate on prostitution

An abundant international debate among researchers and activists has identified transnational prostitution as not only a relationship between two individuals but also a reflection of the profound inequality of class, gender, race and economic relations.[12] Two alliances, with very different viewpoints, have advanced radical critiques of the global system of prostitution and sought to promote solutions that will demolish the system from within. The first starts from the assumption that it is impossible to sell sexual services without losing one's personal dignity, whereas the second recognizes both the full legitimacy and the social value of the labour of prostitution. However, though reflecting different moralities, both try to confront the core of the problem, which is to guarantee real freedom for women. Let us see how they do it.

The first approach, which is based on a more general social critique, calls for intervention to change the nature of the male–female power relations that legitimize prostitution. It recognizes no social legitimacy in prostitution, seeing it instead as a form of oppression historically induced by the uneven distribution of power between men and women that underlies the capitalist social order. Since prostitution is never a free choice but always the result of necessity, any distinction between voluntary and forced prostitution is unacceptable: none of the existing forms of prostitution can help to promote the rights or the status of women, and the grave psychological consequences and physical harm that it causes make it incompatible with human dignity. Female prostitution creates an underclass of women, mostly from backgrounds of family abuse, poor education and low economic opportunity, whose role is to serve the sexual needs of men.

The socially critical approach therefore places the emphasis on the social conditions underlying prostitution as a market phenomenon, and on the behaviour of clients in paying to abuse women. One important aspect of this position is that it holds clients individually responsible, on the grounds that it is their demand which fuels the sex industry and therefore the abuse and trafficking of women. The movement associated with the International Abolitionist Federation and the Coalition against Trafficking in Women maintains that the exponential growth of sex trafficking in recent years has been brought about by the newly permissive attitude towards prostitution. In its view, governments should seriously enforce the existing laws on prostitution, adopt new measures to penalize customers, and direct campaigns of information, and dissuasion, towards potential clients (Leifholdt 1999).

The second approach, which we may describe as functionalist, has two main objectives: to combat forced prostitution, and to eliminate the stigma and discrimination accompanying the practice of prostitution. Arguing that women and men who sell sexual services should be recognized as workers, the movement in question prefers to use the terms 'sex work' and 'sex worker' as a way of avoiding the moral judgement and emotional connotations of the traditional terminology. In this view, sex work is not by definition lacking in dignity: it can even be performed in a reputable manner, and be the result of a free choice (McElroy 2002). For this to be true, however, sex work must fulfil certain criteria: first, the sex worker must be able to negotiate the terms of the exchange and to refuse any particular client or act; second, the sex services must be given in return for payment, in suitable surroundings and without intervention by any third party; and, third, the price of the services must reflect the course of the market, with its prevailing balance of supply and demand (Dottridge 1999). With these minimum conditions, to prostitute oneself does not mean to sell one's person but to sell a service. For some people, then, whether male or female, prostitution can offer greater margins of freedom and autonomy than other occupations, while from a moral point of view it may be considered an economic activity on a par with all others. The selling of sexual services varies considerably in form and significance and does not represent a problem in itself; it becomes a problem when it is not recognized by society and does not enjoy adequate social protection. In reality, with rare exceptions, prostitution is not covered by work and safety regulations: it is nearly always an informal, or even illegal, branch of activity. Improved working conditions for sex workers would therefore have obviously beneficial effects at the level of health and hygiene, and also expose customers to lesser risks of infection. Some public campaigns in India, for example, have shown that well-informed sex workers capable of asserting their rights run ten times less of a risk of HIV and other sexually transmitted diseases than do unorganized prostitutes.

This second approach mainly expresses the point of view of people active in the sex market, whose movement to advance their rights led to the issuing of the Sex Workers Manifesto, at the First National Conference of Sex Workers attended by three thousand people in 1997 in Calcutta (Kempadoo and Doezema 1998). This movement, born in 1975 in France and the United States, has gradually spread around the world and linked up with various independent initiatives, some in developing countries such as India or Thailand where there are strong traditions of prostitution. But, though it has consolidated itself in countries where the sex market has long existed on a large scale, the movement is still in its infancy in parts of the world – especially the ex-Communist countries – that have only recently undergone an exponential growth of prostitution.[13]

Notes

1. The type of prostitution to which Simmel was referring was that practised in so-called 'closed houses'. He took over the prevailing view of prostitution as a 'necessary evil' and considered the prostitute a victim of the moral paradox of society: the commodity she sells, her sexuality, is the most personal thing a woman has, while what she gets in return, money, is the most impersonal object circulating in society (Simmel 1968, 1984).
2. Occasional prostitution by very young people seems quite common all over Europe, where girls and boys give (usually incomplete)

sexual services to older men in return for such things as designer clothing or sunglasses. In Japan, there is actually a name for the custom of prostituting oneself for a designer handbag or other such object: *enjokosai.*

3. For a detailed picture of the exploitation of underage prostitution in Western Europe, see Wolthius, Blaak 2002.

4. In the big cities the proportion of transsexuals and men can be as high as 30 per cent: see Europap/Tampep 2001. For the figures on Britain, see Home Office 2004.

5. See 'Giving the Customer What He Wants', *The Economist,* 14–20 February 1998.

6. See the chapter on informal prostitution and tourism in O'Connell Davidson 1998: 76ff.

7. The market is also being internationalized on the supply side, with the constant influx (and trafficking) of young female immigrants from southern China, Burma, Cambodia, Vietnam and Laos.

8. Some interesting documents presented during the congress by ECPAT International (End Child Prostitution, Child Pornography and Trafficking of Children for Sexual Purposes) and UNICEF, and recently updated, may be found on the ECPAT website.

9. For example, the breakdown between visible and invisible prostitution (the latter referring to that which takes place entirely in closed places) varies considerably from country to country.

10. Salt and Hogarth (2000) have identified twenty-two definitions of trafficking and present them as an attachment to their study; see Kelly (2002) for a full discussion of definitions, as well as Gomez 2001.

11. In Article 3 of the Protocol to Prevent, Suppress and Punish Trafficking in Persons, Especially Women and Children, supplementing the United Nations Convention against Transnational Organized Crime, we read: '"Trafficking in persons" shall mean the recruitment, transportation, transfer, harbouring or receipt of persons, by means of the threat or use of force or other forms of coercion, of abduction, of fraud, of deception, of the abuse of power or of a position of vulnerability or of the giving or receiving of payments or benefits to achieve the consent of a person having control over another person, for the purpose of exploitation. Exploitation shall include, at a minimum, the exploitation of the prostitution of others or other forms of sexual exploitation, forced labour or services,

slavery or practices similar to slavery, servitude or the removal of organs.... The consent of a victim of trafficking in persons to the intended exploitation set forth in subparagraph (a) of this article shall be irrelevant where any of the means set forth in subparagraph (a) have been used' (United Nations 2000).

12. For a history of this debate since the last century, see Stienstra 1996.

13. The first regional conference of sex workers in East-Central Europe took place at Balastya, Hungary, between 8 and 14 April 2000.

2

La donna è mobile:
female emigration and prostitution

The countries of origin

The feminization of poverty

International migration has doubled over the last thirty-five years, and the female component of this has grown considerably. Today, the 50 million or more expatriate women, girls and female children make up nearly half of the total population living temporarily or permanently in other than their country of birth. In about a third of destination countries, the proportion of immigrant women is greater than that of men. The flows to Europe are on average slightly less than 50 per cent female, and above 50 per cent only in the cases of Finland, Belgium, Greece, Portugal and Italy. Although care for the family remains the chief responsibility of immigrant women, worldwide changes mean that many more now leave alone in search of a job, and more and more often their work represents the main source of income for their family (ILO 2004).

For women, as indeed for men, migration is caused either by so-called 'expulsion' factors (grave social-economic crisis, war, other conflicts) or by 'attraction' factors involving a belief that it is possible somewhere else to improve the quality of one's life or that of one's family. Often the decision to leave is not the result of hunger or extreme poverty, but rather of a clash between what the individual expects from life and what is actually available. The relationship between the two undergoes constant modification. In the past decade, rapid changes have taken place in many parts of the world and profoundly affected people's everyday lives. According to material presented by UN Secretary-General Kofi Annan, some positive signs were registered in the 1990s at the global level: for example, the average growth of GDP in developing countries rose from 2.7 per cent to 4.3 per cent. At the same time, however, inequalities grew in the distribution of wealth between various areas, so that today 15 per cent of the population in the rich countries accounts for 56 per cent of global consumption. In many regions, economic growth has occurred without social development, while in others there has been no growth at all. Thus in the so-called 'transition economies', where growth of 1.8 per cent was recorded in the 1980s, the equivalent figure in the 1990s was negative growth of −2.5 per cent. The rate of inflation is currently very high there: 86 per cent in Russia, 44 per cent in Romania, and 43 per cent in the former Yugoslavia. In Russia, at least 60 million people – or 40 per cent of the population – were living below the poverty threshold in the year 2000. In Africa, the situation is growing steadily worse, and consumption is down 20 per cent on the level of twenty-five years ago. In Nigeria, for example, per capita GNP is twenty times lower than in Italy. In the words of Kofi Annan, 'globalization has strikingly shown its volatility. Many countries have derived benefits from it, but others have paid a very high price as they have been shaken by serious financial crises' (Annan 2002).

According to UN estimates, women today make up a majority of the world's poor: some 70 per cent of those living below the poverty threshold are female. Of these, a high proportion face growing difficulties, in a paradoxical situation where they have to keep their own children, or parents, yet are discriminated against in the labour market. In the former Soviet countries, Latin America, Africa and Asia, women get much lower wages than men – and the world average is little more than 50 per cent, according to UN figures. Moreover, it is usually women who, through their care work in the family, make up for the effects of sudden economic and social changes, bearing the brunt of the crisis or failure of social welfare systems. In large parts of the world this dynamic – which goes by the name of the 'feminization of poverty'[1] – has been unleashed by the economic privatization that accompanies the advance of globalization. In Latin America and Eastern Europe, the redistribution of resources due to privatization in the past fifteen years has mainly hit women, by depriving them of collective goods and social services. The American scholar Louis Shelley gives a clear illustration of this:

> The former Soviet Union has gone from a society that was 100 percent state owned to a lower level of state ownership in the economy than you have in countries such as Italy or Mexico that have had state interventionist economies. In that period of transition, the resources of the state were privatized primarily to men. After the initial privatization, which was so improperly handled that it brought almost no resources to the state, no revenues were being paid and nothing was being done to provide social services to women, education for children, summer schools, and so forth. So a simultaneous impoverishment of women occurred, not only in their salaries and their access to property but also to social services. (Shelley 2000: 6)

To grasp what is specific, and peculiarly vulnerable, about female migratory flows, let us look more closely at two very different regions: the former Soviet republics, especially Russia and

Ukraine; and an African country, Nigeria. These are countries from which large numbers of women leave to work in the sex markets.

The case of Russia and the ex-Soviet regions

In Russia the rise of the market economy has brought huge changes in lifestyle and a growing tendency for women to emigrate, including for short periods of time. Official sources are unable to give a precise figure for the hundreds of thousands of women who leave the country temporarily, because they do not always do this through regular channels. Temporary emigration is generally undertaken to solve problems arising from the shortage of jobs and the crisis of the public assistance system. Data concerning the lifestyle of women present a very negative picture. With regard to work, 70 per cent of Russian women – whose educational level is among the highest in the world – said in 1997 that they could find no work suited to their vocational training (Caldwell, Galster and Steinzor 1997). A large percentage of women currently do not have economic security from a job of their own; they are often employed in informal activities or domestic labour, and Ministry of Labour figures report that 70 per cent of the unemployed are female. In St Petersburg, the wages of female employees are on average 43 per cent of those earned by men. Surveys conducted in Russia and among Russians living abroad have also shown that women have difficulty finding a job unless they agree to 'entertain' their boss sexually (Nurmi 2000: 6). Problems of sexual harassment at the workplace are widespread, and there is still no law that specifically punishes such conduct. As to the family world, cuts in services to the elderly, education and health have had a major impact on the daily lives of mothers and daughters, who often have to care for the family alone. Young mothers, in particular,

Sex Traffic

who are no longer entitled to the three years' maternity leave on a modest allowance that applied in the Soviet Union, often find themselves having to face great hardship. One major problem comes from the high rate of alcoholism among young men. Over the past decade, the proportion of single mothers with children has risen considerably: studies published in November 2001 by the Russian Academy of Sciences reveal that a third of children (twice as many as ten years before) are born to unmarried women. And lastly, perhaps in part because women are so little represented in organs of government, politicians and the justice system pay very little attention to cases of violence against women. In 2002, the Russian report to the committee of CEDAW (United Nations Convention on the Elimination of All Forms of Discrimination Against Women) stated that each year at least 14,000 women were killed by members of their family. Yet, despite the gravity of the problem, the lack of resources means that there are few shelters for victims of domestic violence. NGOs speak of a general indifference to the issue, and report great mental suffering in large sections of the female population, including a widespread lack of self-esteem and loss of hope for the future. Social workers stress that many women are resigned to take unskilled but relatively well paid jobs abroad, in the belief that the change might improve their conditions of life; for the youngest among them, one of the main incentives to emigrate is the search for (not only economic) independence and emancipation. Girls, in fact, find themselves in a paradoxical situation: they long for equal opportunities with men, and take the Western model as their ideal, but they face a society that heavily discriminates against women, and post-Communist governments that make propaganda for the traditional model of the family.

The preconditions for a sharp rise in female emigration, albeit in varying forms, have been created in all the countries of the former Soviet Union. It is estimated that throughout this region more than 120 million persons earn less than $4 a day. In Ukraine, where the average wage is $30 a month, 60 per cent of the unemployed and 80 per cent of people who have lost their job since 1991 are female (Hughes 2000b; Levchenko 1999). According to UN estimates, at least half a million young people there are prepared to emigrate without proper assurances, and are therefore liable to be heavily exploited in foreign labour markets. The Ukrainian authorities have reported the spread of organized trafficking of young women, who feed the matrimonial business and practices involving extreme exploitation in foreign black markets, porn networks and prostitution rackets (Bradanini 1999; Gorbunova 1999).

More generally, the United Nations estimates that each year at least 500,000 women leave the countries of the former Soviet Union – most notably, Moldova, Ukraine and Russia, but also Belarus, Georgia and Kazakhstan – and end up in high-exploitation labour markets (UNDP 1999: 89). Most people leaving these regions know they will have to face very difficult situations, and the statistics are indeed quite disturbing. A recent survey, based on interviews with 3,000 people in the former Soviet countries, showed that there is an acute awareness of the problem of trafficking: in the Urals region 28 per cent of respondents said that one female relative or close friend of theirs had been a victim of it, while the corresponding figure in Armenia was 32 per cent and in the eastern regions 25 per cent. Most of the women had been tricked in their own country, usually after answering an advertisement and being chosen for employment through a long process of interviews, meetings and photo exchanges. Once abroad, they were cheated, duped and exploited beyond anything one can imagine. Yet, despite widespread knowledge of the risks, a full 74 per cent of girls between 10 and 19, and 67 per cent of women between 19 and 29, still thought of emigration as a great opportunity and expressed serious ambitions to work abroad (Mira Med Institute 1999).

The case of Nigeria

In Nigeria, too, the awareness of risks is not sufficient to rid young and very young women of a wish to emigrate, nor, above all, of a feeling that it is necessary. Female emigration to Western countries has been fuelled here in recent years by the sharpening of social-economic contradictions, which, though different from those affecting the former Soviet Union, have had equally negative effects on women's lives. The first sizeable flow of Nigerian women to Europe, in the late 1980s, coincided with the beginning of the structural adjustment programme inside the country; it mainly consisted of young women from urban middle strata who had been unable to prevent a sharp fall in their standard of living. They decided to take the path of emigration when the rate of female unemployment reached danger point. Without realizing it, they thus became the 'pioneers' of a migration chain in which, as we shall see, thousands upon thousands of young women became steered and directed by ever fiercer criminal organizations. This flow soon became more diffuse, in both sociological and geographical origin, involving not only educated and liberated women but growing numbers of half-illiterate girls, who in some cases were forced to leave by their families. Now rural areas in southern Nigeria are the most affected, while the main destination countries in Europe are Italy, Belgium and the Netherlands, as well as Britain, France and Spain. A recent study has shown that in many villages of southern Nigeria, where pockets of great social backwardness remain, parents still have a very strong influence over their daughters' lives and generally decide when and whom they marry. The coordinator of the research group pointed out that, in these regions, extreme poverty drives many heads of families to think that the only chance of survival, or at least the only way of reducing the scale of the poverty, is to send their own daughters, sisters or mothers to work abroad.[2] Although in Nigeria 70 per cent of women contribute through work to the family economy, female labour is in most cases underpaid. More generally, the conditions of life are hard for many Nigerians: a long period of corrupt rule by military juntas led to the present situation where 40 per cent of the population live below the poverty line, and the country's infrastructure – health service, schools and drinking water supply – is woefully inadequate. Many impecunious families do not send their daughters to school, and as a result two-thirds of the female population are illiterate (UNDP 1999).

Opportunities to work abroad

'Informal' labour markets and migrant trafficking

Although it is the situation in the home country that drives people to emigrate, it is also true that migration is often a result of the play of supply and demand. The growing numbers who leave the poorer countries for economically dynamic parts of the world indicate that there is a surplus supply of workers but also a strong demand for their services in the destination countries.

In general, the governments in destination countries continue to obstruct legal forms of entry and, indirectly, to favour the spread of informal labour markets and the exploitation of immigrants whose papers are not in order. But, far from being seen as an obstacle, the existence of such a 'grey area' may actually encourage would-be immigrants to set out without the necessary work permit (Ghosh 1998). The phenomenon is difficult to quantify. The ILO estimates that between 10 and 15 per cent of migrants in the world (not all in the developed countries) are in an irregular situation, and that they face 'grave risks for their human rights and basic liberties when they are recruited or employed outside the law' (ILO 2004). According to this UN agency, working conditions for a large number of migrants are marked by abuse and exploitation and sometimes even forms of forced labour; they are too often denied the right to join a union and exposed to discriminatory or xenophobic attitudes. The informal economy, which has been growing not only in developing countries but also in Europe and North America, employs more and more men, women and minors at levels of pay, in conditions of work and safety, and for a number of working hours that do not correspond to the negotiated norms; employers are thus riding roughshod over their rights in a number of ways. Everywhere in the world, immigrants in an irregular situation tend to form a special category of people at high risk of extreme exploitation, since they do not enjoy the same rights as citizens of the host country.

We have seen that independent female migration tends to grow with the crisis of the local economy, and with women's increased responsibility for the economic survival of their family. Whatever the initial impetus, however, emigration takes place in a context of huge obstacles. For so-called 'globalization' is based on a paradox: the liberalization of international markets is not matched by a liberalization of the movement of persons or labour-power. Goods move ever more cheaply, along swift and secure channels, but people face ever greater difficulties. In developed countries, and not only there, the last two decades have witnessed a gradual tightening of immigration policy. In the case of Europe, this trend became evident in the second half of the 1970s, and in recent years – partly through the creation of a common Schengen area that more and more countries have joined – the EU's external frontier controls have become more and more thorough and modernized.

Meanwhile, it has become increasingly difficult to obtain an entry visa for many countries in the world. The result is that today, in all continents, a large sector of international migration takes place outside the law, and therefore in the absence of legal safeguards. In some areas – for example, the 'Eurasian Economic Union' made up of Tajikistan, Kirghistan, Kazakhstan, the Russian Federation and Belarus (IOM 2001f) – 99 per cent of migration for the purpose of work takes place in an irregular manner. The emigrants – or migrants, as they are now usually called, to underline their insecurity and frequent movement – have to face tortuous journeys that sometimes put their lives at risk. Their country of origin often raises problems about the granting of permission to emigrate, while the destination country imposes ever more stringent requirements for visas and residence permits, and widespread corruption in embassies, consulates and frontier checkpoints hugely increases the costs of the trip. This often means that it can be contemplated only by someone able to pay large sums of money.

All over the world, intermediaries and traffickers make it possible for men and women to embark on the difficult journey, either by smoothing the way for them to be given a permit or by organizing a trip illegally (Salt and Stein 1997). Veritable underground networks have sprung up in this way. Hovering around the embassies of the world's richest countries are traffickers whose access to corrupt channels, forgers and travel agencies enables them to collect the necessary documents and visas, real or fake. In Europe alone – where at least 400,000 people are thought to enter illegally each year, with or without the help of traffickers – the Europol police agency estimates the annual turnover of this business at €1 billion.[3]

The longest and riskiest journeys are organized in minute detail. We now know that, in China, the Philippines, Africa or the former Soviet republics, traffickers are capable of planning trips that last more than six months, in varying degrees of danger (Monzini 2000, 2003). The routes are well worked out, and traffickers may be able to guarantee, for example, that they will try another way if the original plan does not succeed. At the various stages, they actively work with all kinds of people such as forgers, experienced palm-greasers, drivers, guides, sailors and guards, the services in question being sold dear to the migrant even for the shortest trips. The customer usually begins to pay the trafficker for them before departure, and concludes the deal once he or she has arrived in the agreed destination country. To take one example, according to the International Organization for Migration, the average charges for entry to Europe from the Dominican Republic are between $4,000 and $10,000, and from China $10,000 to $15,000, while the rate from North Africa to Spain is usually between $2,200 and $3,500. The journey from the Philippines to the USA or Canada, including false travel documents, a passport and entry visa, costs from $4,000 to $8,000 (Leones and Caparas 2002).

The organizations handling these trips may take the form of travel or employment agencies, customs clearance services or passenger transport companies, or else be without any definite structure. As in any business, their trustworthiness varies a great deal. But the illegal character of the operations makes it easier to swindle the customer; things do not always go as planned. A cruel trick may sometimes be played regarding the final destination, as in that episode from the late nineteenth century when people were taken on board a ship supposedly bound for America and then dumped among what seemed to be cowboys, only on the Maremma coast of Tuscany. Thousands of migrants from Asia today find themselves landing not in Western Europe, as they had planned, but in Africa, Albania or Tunisia.

Human trafficking also intertwines with the organization of illegal labour markets (Ruggiero 1997). In general, there is not a simple equation: migrant trafficking equals exploitation, even if the overlap between the two can be so great that they are indistinguishable. In any case, they are treated differently from a legal point of view: the former is considered a crime against the state, since it involves a violation of its frontiers; the latter is a crime against the individual and human dignity.

The typical case of trafficking that involves a kind of slavery is that of intermediaries who, whether under cover of an agency or on their own account, deal with various problems facing an individual (the need for official documents and organized travel, a loan to buy the visa and pay for the trip, definite prospects of a job, etc.) and offer solutions that turn out to be simply fraudulent. Anyone who puts their trust in an unknown intermediary has little ability to assess the worth of what he proposes. To reduce the risk, emigrants usually choose an intermediary on the recommendation of relatives or friends, or else explore several options before they select the most convincing. But there are also cases where a professional scout directly persuades someone to leave, using ways of making initial contact between 'client' and 'trafficker' that differ from country to country. Of course, given the nature of the respective labour markets, the danger of being trapped in circuits of exploitation is much greater for women who emigrate without proper documents than it is for men in the same situation.

The international female labour market

Recent research has clearly shown that female emigrants throughout the world find their main opportunities in 'typically female' labour markets (Wijers and Lap-Chew 1997). This is a fact of life everywhere: for women who leave with their papers in order and for those who leave without papers, for women with a high level of education and for illiterate women. As experts in the field have pointed out, a tiny proportion find employment as unskilled workers in small or medium-sized firms (for example, in textiles or woollen goods, or the clothing or food sector), and an even tinier proportion in white-collar jobs or some form of intellectually demanding occupation. To an extent that varies little internationally, the majority of female migrants are employed in personal services or the tertiary sector. Apart from domestic labour, the main sectors that take on women are catering (as waitresses, dishwashers, barmaids), the fashion industry (models, hairdressers, seamstresses), the diverse entertainment industry (escorts, strippers, hostesses in day or night clubs) and prostitution.

Migration female-style is usually more prone to deception, not because women are weaker than men or more gullible by nature, but because they have fewer opportunities. The labour market, in a sometimes distorted and often magnified way, reproduces the gender discrimination that women have already encountered in their country of origin. Large areas of the labour markets intended for women are structured in an informal manner that allows great scope for exploitation. As regards domestic labour, demand has shot up in both Europe and the United States, as public childcare and senior-care facilities have failed to keep pace with the massively increasing number of women at work outside the home and the rising average age of the population. In America, for instance, where it is estimated that women are the main or sole income-earner in more than a half of families, they are in no position to deal with all the housekeeping and childcare (Ehrenreich and Hochschild 2002: 9). Domestic labour everywhere has strong aspects of irregularity or illegality, and official regulatory policies in the destination countries are widely disregarded. There are thought to be millions of women in the world who work in this sector and face unfavourable conditions, ranging from poor pay and long hours through humiliating treatment to forms of straightforward servitude. Here labour flexibility reigns supreme: supply and demand meet in an informal, irregular manner, with no protection for the civil rights of immigrant women, who often lack and continue to lack residence permits. Whereas, in the case of prostitution, trafficking and new forms of slavery are becoming widely noted and challenged, much less is known about them in the sector of domestic labour.[4]

The harshest systems of exploitation, however, are organized in the world of commercial sex. There are two reasons for this: it is the sector where women are least protected, and it is the most profitable sector for those who exploit them. The rates for sexual services are incomparably higher than for any of the other sectors of female activity mentioned above. According to Interpol estimates, the exploitation of a woman in the cheapest sectors of prostitution in Western Europe brings in some €120,000 to €150,000 a year (Bradanini 1999). Exploiters able to keep 70–90 per cent of the earnings of three intensively worked street or brothel prostitutes can make an average of €2,100 to €3,300 a day.

Entry into the commercial sex circuits

The decision to leave

As we have seen, in many countries of the world, the circuits in which young immigrant women prostitute themselves are controlled by various kinds of criminal groups and pimps, who have developed a degree of 'expertise' and a capacity to impose their will through violence. But how do women fall victim to this system in the first place? The women most heavily exploited by criminals have not all been kidnapped and raped. Their trajectory is often structurally much more complex, so much so that it may at first appear contradictory, or hard to understand, for those who continue to think in terms of innocents brutally turned into 'fallen women' (Stienstra 1996). In general, a woman or girl comes into contact with various intermediaries, who, through assorted forms of trickery, fuel her hopes, encourage her to enter their group, and then make it impossible for her to find a way out.

But it would be wrong to throw the whole weight of explanation on the criminal element. To grasp the full complexity, it is first of all essential to realize that young women who enter the prostitution circuits have a strong wish to change their life by leaving for a distant country. Interviews with female victims of trafficking show that some are duped about the nature of the work that awaits them, and that others accept they will have to work in the entertainment or prostitution sector.[5] The attempt to find social and economic emancipation, either for themselves or for their family, is always the central element in their decision to leave. The precise origin of the desire for change may vary: very often it is a situation of grave economic hardship, perhaps involving the need to support young children, ailing parents or a brother or sister; sometimes, as social workers report, it is a background of great loneliness stemming from abuse, life in orphanages, parental alcoholism, incest or serious psychological problems. To leave and work in a foreign country, in a vaguely defined sector of sexual entertainment, may be a voluntary decision, taken alone or even with the support of the family. All women are aware of the dangers and the unknowns, but the objective need to escape a condition of great social-economic or psychological hardship, together with the 'attractiveness' of highly paid entertainment work that seems to open up new prospects in life, are powerful forces driving them to leave.

In the so-called 'transition countries', where until recently prostitution scarcely existed and was considered a taboo area, and in countries like Nigeria that offer women very few prospects, work abroad in the entertainment or the prostitution sector may be seen as an opportunity. But this material opportunity is not experienced as such within the cultural codes and prevailing modes of conduct of countries of origin which have benefited from sizeable remittances sent home by many thousands of women around the world; here, work in entertainment, and *a fortiori* sex work, are considered morally reprehensible and bear a social stigma. Studies in some countries, however, have shown a psychological and cultural background among very young potential recruits that makes them increasingly prepared to accept work as an entertainer.

One survey of attitudes to migration in urban areas of Ukraine (one of the countries most heavily involved in trafficking) has recorded precisely this aspect (IOM 1998). The interviews with women and girls between 15 and 35 years of age show that 40 per cent have a strong inclination to go abroad, even if this means leaving without solid support and exposing themselves to the risks of trafficking, but not one of them says that an offer of work in the sex industry would be acceptable. However, to leave to become a dancer or entertainer – which is not considered acceptable by older women – seems an attractive idea to all the girls between 15 and 17. Younger generations do not in principle rule out becoming an entertainer, and earning a lot of money, far from the eyes of their friends, acquaintances and relatives. The survey results indicate a strong desire for change, but also suggest that people in Ukraine are not yet very familiar with how such activity is organized abroad. The girls do not see clearly that the lines of demarcation between the entertainment and prostitution sectors are highly tenuous for someone arriving without resources, or, more especially, that their expectations are quite remote from the reality of work in this field. They tend to be persuaded by those who talk them into the business. Their hope is to meet rich, elegant men and to have the opportunity of leading a different life in another country, or perhaps to make sacrifices for a while and then return home with a solid basis for the future. Such expectations are a powerful impetus in the decision to leave. Most girls think that their understanding with people linked in to foreign work circuits considerably reduces the margin of uncertainty and offers them some assurances about the activity in which they will be expected to engage. What they do not see is that a high price is always paid for such 'protection'. In the end, therefore, the entertainment work that they imagine to be an instrument of emancipation turns out to be the exact opposite; their free choice becomes a forced entry into the world of prostitution, as their initial expectations are dashed in a place far from home.

Another, by no means secondary, aspect needs to be emphasized here. The cultural implications are such that the women in question usually pay a much higher emotional price than they expected to reach the destination on which they have pinned their hopes. Once there, apart from the treatment in store for them, they often have to come to terms with a major separation from their family, who know nothing of the kind of work they will be doing. As social workers point out, even if the women manage to send money home, they often find themselves breaking the relationship of trust and confidence with their family; it seems an insurmountable problem to tell other members of the family about how they are treated, and in general they flatly reject any idea of sharing their own sufferings. As one Lithuanian girl asked, what is the point of explaining your situation to someone back home who can anyway do very little? The communication problem may express itself in a potentially disastrous inability to ask for help, even in the gravest circumstances. Socially isolated, deprived of the basic emotional resources of their circle of family and friends, the newly arrived women become much more vulnerable to pimps and their blackmail tactics.

Recruitment and deception

The ways of recruiting women in their country of origin are roughly the same as those used in the 'white slave trade' of the nineteenth century. Recruiters know how to employ various forms of trickery, which may sometimes be adapted to a woman's particular culture or the context in which the approach is made. From information collected in Europe, it would seem that a number of options are available: in Belgium, for example, in 59 per cent of the 162 cases studied it was the recruiter who approached the victim, while in 22 per cent it was the victim who took the initiative by making the first contact. In 61 per cent of cases the recruiter was someone unknown to the victim, in 13 per cent someone known, in 10 per cent the woman's partner, and 9 per cent a friend (Vandeckerckhove et al. 2003). More particularly, a Dutch study has described the three main techniques used in luring women from Eastern Europe to the local prostitution market: deception about the conditions of work, deception about the nature of the work, and kidnapping (Vocks and Nijboer 2000). In varying proportions, these techniques may be found in all the countries of origin. Let us look at them more closely.

Unlike in the case of some countries, such as Italy, the most frequent means of trafficking girls to the Netherlands is deception about the conditions of work. Most of the women and girls in question knew when they left that they would be working as prostitutes, for the highly developed Dutch sex industry has an international reputation that strongly attracts women intending to work in this field. But the working conditions turn out to be very different from what was originally promised. The young women mostly come from families with serious problems, have received little education, and have sometimes already had experience of prostitution. Usually they trust an intermediary already known to them; in fact, the commonest means of deception is through a male friend or acquaintance. Another reason why they are trustful is that they do not have much to lose – and also, of course, because they do not imagine their journey will involve beatings and threats in which they are treated as merchandise. The obligation to repay the travel debt may then lead to total loss of control over their movements, so that they find themselves in an unknown country, at the mercy of alien people who speak a different language in which they are hard put to communicate.

Cases of deception about the actual nature of the work abroad are more common among young middle-class women who have been doing menial work in their home country. Faced with difficult living conditions, such individuals are easily susceptible to attractive offers of work abroad and may decide to leave with no help from anyone except perhaps an unknown intermediary; the risks they run are so much the greater because they have neither contacts nor sufficient savings to make their own way abroad. The so-called 'lover boy' recruitment method is widespread: a man seduces a girl by promising her marriage and a rosy future and, once abroad, either sells her or forces her (through love or violence) into prostitution, making her the prisoner of a relationship based on psychological submission and economic dependence.[6] Now that this has been highlighted as the typical method of trafficking, however, it no longer seems to have the same force as before. A recent study of Romanian girls, for example, shows that their usual image of a trafficker is precisely of a good-looking, rich and unmarried foreigner. If the trafficker has a different profile, this is most likely to be when she is a woman and able to succeed better because of the fewer suspicions that this arouses (Lazaroiu and Alexandru 2003: 6off.). Thus, in countries where the 'lover boy' figure was most common (the Balkans, especially Albania), female recruiters are now a growing phenomenon. They are women who, having once been victims of exploitation themselves, try to make a career by becoming recruiters and controllers of new girls; for example, they return to their country of origin to convince girls they know to go abroad with them, by tricking them about the nature of the work in store. The example they set of a successful woman seems very encouraging and means that their offers are readily taken up.

These figures play quite an important role in ensuring the continuity of flows, both because they are later able to blackmail the women by drawing on knowledge of their personal situation back home, and because the sense of great proximity due to shared origins can be very useful in creating ties of psychological dependence. Recruitment in the home country, which often occurs in small groups to lend support, may also take place through other channels. Agents and agencies hold out the prospect of work as entertainers or models, prestigious artistic or professional careers, employment as cooks, babysitters or home helps, and even marriage opportunities abroad.[7] Job offers may be passed on by word of mouth or through advertisements in newspapers and handbills, or on the Internet and local television. This system, already in use in Southeast Asia (for example, the Philippines: see UNODC 2003), began to take shape in Russia and Ukraine a decade or so ago and has recently been spreading throughout East-Central Europe and the Balkans.

A typical advertisement in a newspaper reads: 'Educated, well-mannered women under thirty sought for work in modern office abroad. 600 dollars a month, documents and travel included.' In Ukraine it is estimated that 20 per cent of the women are recruited through the press or television: an examination of local newspapers turned up at least twenty suspect ads in each one. Often, friends or acquaintances pass on the word (either in good faith or for interested motives) and tell women how to contact the agencies.

There are also recruiters who work in public places or go from
door to door – mostly women, who receive a reward of $200 to
$6,000 for each girl they recruit (Hughes 2000b: 6–11). In many
cases, the existence of an agency is necessary to persuade the
girls that the offer of work abroad is genuine; a formal selection
procedure, involving several meetings, informal parties, personal
files, photographic sessions and the compilation of a photographic
portfolio, can prove very convincing. Most agencies work closely
with nightclub 'impresarios' (to whom the girls are handed over
soon after arrival in the destination country) or with traffickers (to
whom they are handed over, or sold, after crossing the frontier).
An eloquent case is that of Irina, who lost her father as a child and
managed to reach university only with great difficulty. A woman
she met said she was a tour manager and invited her to become
her assistant in France for two months, on a high salary. Irina
decided to leave, but their trip was soon cut short. She was sold
in Romania, raped and taken to an illegal brothel in Germany,
then to another one in Italy, where she remained for three months
before managing to escape.[8]

The previously mentioned Dutch study identifies two distinct
kinds of kidnapping, a not so frequent occurrence. The first
category involves especially attractive girls who do not have a
pressing economic or other need to go abroad. They are first
approached in a bar or disco, on the street or some other public
place; a professional recruiter then drugs or seduces them, takes
them across the frontier and holds them in captivity. The second
category consists of prostitutes without a family, who, though
having no intention to emigrate, are sold by their pimp and set
to work in the international market.

Another dynamic, not identified in the Dutch study, is very
widespread outside Eastern Europe – in Nigeria and Southeast
Asia, but also the Balkans. Here, the family convinces a young

woman to leave and seek her fortune abroad. It is not unusual for a girl's own parents to send her to Europe or the United States, at great sacrifice to themselves, or to look for a professional recruiter. In the latter case, the girl does not consent but is forced to leave: it is not an individual choice that she makes. The family, which is not aware of the methods of exploitation abroad, incurs a debt with a publicly known figure in the community in order to cover the costs of the daughter's trip, but in reality that person is either a skilled speculator or receives an advance on what the girl will make from prostitution. Here too, then, deception underlies the contract and the decision to leave: deception about the nature or conditions of the work (UNICRI 2003b; Southeast Asia Watch 1998; Renton 2001).

To complete the picture, we should mention that some women who go abroad independently may be gradually inserted into the circuits of intensive exploitation. They may, for example, resort to prostitution to solve economic problems in their host country (most often, the need to pay off their debt from the original trip to Europe, the USA or elsewhere, which has left them trapped in terrible relations of usury). Interviews with such women show that they are most likely to see prostitution as a temporary solution at the point when the few months of their tourist visa run out and they find themselves in an irregular situation vis-à-vis the authorities. Talens (2001) reports the case of a woman from the Dominican Republic who intended to work as a home help in Spain, but who had had to pay several thousand dollars to cover the costs of the trip and the necessary documents. To amass this sum, she had sold her possessions and passed the hat around her family and friends, but also incurred loans at a usurious rate of between 20 and 30 per cent a month. When her permit to stay in Spain expired, she had two ways to finish paying off the debt: either she could remain there illegally until she had earned enough money, or she could return home, ask for a second loan and leave again, having run up a still higher burden of debt. It is this kind of pressure that induces young women to enter the circle of entertainment and paid sex. In other words, debt pressure and fear of deportation may at any moment lead them to accept an offer from a skilled intermediary to introduce them to the world of prostitution, at the maximum profit to himself.

Subjugation

In general, it is after a trip that women are inserted into the circle of exploitation. Their crossing of the frontier may be illegal, but it may also be legal, with genuine or forged documents, or involve some combination of the two that depends on how well their accompaniers are organized. Some journeys are planned in the finest detail: for example, the movement of three Mexican girls to an illegal brothel in Texas, or the airline travel of several young Thai women to a massage parlour in Paris. In these cases, the owner of the establishment in question takes direct charge of the women and keeps their documents, explains the nature and methods of the work assigned to them, and makes it clear that they will be required to pay back the money spent on their acquisition, plus an extra sum on top. Of course, the agreements are imposed with the help of blackmail and assorted threats. The routes are established well in advance, and the traffickers put up the costs of the trip in anticipation of repayment with interest.

More complex cases involve a graduated network, where the recruiters hand over women to traffickers, who pay to accompany them on a section of the journey, without placing them in sex markets and without using blackmail or violence. Once over the frontier, these traffickers deliver them to other individuals in return for a sum greater than they originally paid: girls for cash. There may thus be several transition points. The girls do

not suddenly find out that they are destined for the forced prostitution market, and so they trustingly continue their journey to
the unknown country. The delivery price varies with the type
of market on which the women are sold, reaching a maximum
where the profits are likely to be greatest. The actual mechanism
is simple: at each point along the way, the price of the woman
increases, and so does the amount of the debt she will have to pay
back to her purchaser; each intermediary thus makes a satisfactory
income from each handover. The girl's precise value depends on
her looks, but also on the degree of her docility and reliability.
At a certain point, when they are already a long way from home,
the girls are sold to traffickers acting on behalf of the final buyer,
the one who will be entitled to exploit them. In Belgrade or
Bucharest they may well be sold to traffickers operating in London
or Turkey; in Vietnam they may be sold to Shanghai, or Bangkok,
without being able to choose for themselves. In these markets, a
young woman who has already been 'broken in' and psychologically prepared for low-priced prostitution is worth more than a
new recruit of the same age, who is still in several respects an
unknown quantity. The 'breaking-in' process usually takes place
after she is handed over to professionals skilled in various forms
and degrees of violence. The first stage, which makes the victim
immediately vulnerable, is the confiscation of her passport or
travel documents; traffickers and exploiters nearly always do this
to ensure that she does not run away, since it greatly weakens her
position in the destination country and makes her much warier of
seeking the help of the authorities. Apart from the danger of being
reported to the police, actual violence is used to bring home to the
victim the terrible consequences of any attempt to escape. In the
case of women coming from a traditional background, blackmail
based on dishonour is a widely used practice: the threat to tell
their family, or home community, about the real nature of their

work abroad is usually enough to keep them in a state of total subjection. But, as both victims and social workers report, the psychological effects of brutality are immediate; the women are at first unable to believe that they have been sold, refuse to accept their new condition, and try to fight back against the demands of their would-be exploiters. This always leads to acts of humiliation, beatings, ice-cold showers, confinement in a room, deprivation of food, sexual violence – until the girl sees that there is no alternative and, to avoid further mistreatment, stops resisting and subjects herself to the alien will. She waits. When she understands that autonomy, free choice and control over her own fate are no longer possible, she gives in, adapts to the new conditions of life and keeps going as best she can.[9]

For women sold in this way, and trapped in the mechanism of debt, the journeys may be very long and frequent. And, once they reach a new destination, they are often forced to continue travelling, in accordance with a model of itinerant exploitation. Albanian gangs in Greece and Italy, for example, stop off in places with 'their' women for no more than a year at a time. Always on the lookout for bigger profits, they move on a seasonal basis among various regions or countries of Europe, or else force the women to move and swap them around with other gangs. A similar system of national or international rotation also operates in northern Europe, where prostitution takes place only indoors, in clubs, go-go bars or illegal brothels. Here, networks of traffickers specialize in importing girls and then switching them among various places that belong to local exploiters. The types of girl, and the kinds of agreement or price, are obviously different on each market: high-class hotels require more expensive and sophisticated girls, whereas street pimps and the owners of cheap brothels can get away with paying much less. In each case the continual rotation of prostitutes, known as the 'carousel system', increases customer satisfaction. The shifting of girls from bars and night clubs to apartments, saunas and escort services is organized in the most efficient manner, as it is also in the United States or Japan. For the purchasers like to have new girls all the time. Tattooing of the women is another way of confirming that they are subject to a clear-cut authority, for it has been discovered in northern Europe that the bodily mark makes it easier to identify a woman as belonging to a certain 'stable'.

Notes

1. For an analysis of this concept and a presentation of the data, see Baden 1999.
2. See 'Grace against Prostitution', *The News: Middle East Intelligence Wire*, 20 March 2000.
3. *Der Standard* (Vienna), 27 May 1999.
4. See Cabral 2001; Ehrenreich and Hochschild 2002: 145–57.
5. These considerations are based on numerous interviews that I have conducted myself and on corroborating evidence from many other studies in the field. See, for example, the various IOM studies, which always focus in part on this aspect.
6. For a description of this kind of situation, and of the wide range of possible relations between prostitute and pimp, see Barry 1979: 86–120.
7. Criminal organizations use marriage agencies as cover for trafficking operations, or as a way of trapping women who are thinking of emigrating. On the practice of arranged marriages, which often border on recruitment for the prostitution markets, see Lloyd 2000.
8. Interview conducted in Milan, October 2001.
9. Stories of traumatic inductions of this kind have appeared since the early 1990s in the reports of NGOs and international organizations. See especially the publications of Human Rights Watch and the IOM.

3

The mechanisms of the trade

Dynamics

The networks

In the past fifteen years, expansion of the sector of low-priced prostitution has been largely fuelled by the activities of criminal 'networks' specializing in the cross-frontier transport, subjugation and exploitation of women. This has been possible above all because criminal 'pioneers' found favourable terrain in the destination countries: strong demand for cut-price prostitution, and little official reaction to the phenomena associated with exploitation. Criminals gradually took a share of local prostitution markets, either by expanding ones already in existence or by creating new ones, and in this way built up their circuits into a veritable transnational business. According to studies conducted in the early 1990s, the first organized rings sprang up to exploit women from Asia, especially Thailand and the Philippines, and from Latin America, especially the Dominican Republic and Brazil (Barry 1995). Today's markets, unlike those of the 1970s or 1980s, include women from all parts of the world. The currents bringing them have grown more diverse: rings that exploit Filipino or Thai or Latin American women are flanked by others, varying considerably in structure and dimensions, which mainly exploit women from Africa and the former Soviet republics. According to Europol, although traffickers often come from the same country as their victims, there is a growing trend towards cooperation among groups from different backgrounds (Europol 2004). Sometimes the rings traffic women of one specific nationality, sometimes they are able to handle flows from different countries at the same time. UN reports show that the most frequent nationalities of traffickers are, in descending order, Russian, Nigerian, Ukrainian and Albanian (Kangaspunta 2003: 99). Some of the networks have connections in several countries and continents and operate with different structures, since the context of the business itself differs culturally and economically and in its mode of political regulation. The results are everywhere apparent: in the United States and Europe, in China and Japan, local networks offering the services of girls from a single background (Thai or East European, for example) exist alongside places where the customer can often choose among Moldovan, Turkish, Filipino and Ghanaian girls. Before we look at the forms of exploitation prevalent in the destination countries, it would be useful to say a few words about the gradual spread of trafficking networks and the origins and evolution of the transit of women.

Kelly (2002: 8) has identified three general backgrounds to the traffic in women: previous relations of colonial domination or relations of supremacy/dependence between two countries; the power of attraction of certain sex markets; and the profitability of exploitation given the price differential for sexual services between nearby countries. A further source of new cross-border trafficking is certainly the sharp rise in certain long-distance migratory flows. In recent years, relations of slavery-like exploitation designed to extract high profits from prostitution have gained a foothold in large ethnic enclaves: for example, Russians in Israel or the United States, or Chinese in the USA and London. As in the 'white slave trade' of the late nineteenth century, women are initially placed at the disposal of migrant workers, then inserted into wider circuits designed for a local clientele.

If we consider the formation and evolution of these flows, we can see that the various sources have slowly come together in a single global network. The first networks were undoubtedly those born out of neocolonial relations between countries, or relations of interdependence or trade reflected in the structure of the sex industry, and paved the way for more complex forms of trafficking. Thus, as we have already seen, thousands of women from Thailand began to be inserted into the sex markets of the USA and Japan after the development of a local Thai sex market due to the Vietnam War. The flows from Thailand then began to divide, moving towards countries with more lucrative sex markets, such as the Netherlands or Germany, Scandinavia or Australia. Sex tourism brought similar movements elsewhere, as women from the countries on tourist routes were gradually drawn to sex markets in the tourists' countries of origin. Especially since the beginning of the 1990s, tourism has opened up new contacts and created the prerequisites for sexual exploitation, and trafficking, from places in Asia, Africa and Latin America (Ehrenreich, Russell and Hochschild 2002). In this way the Dominican Republic, for example, had by the 1980s already become one of the main sources of women working abroad as prostitutes, and today it is estimated that at least 50,000 Dominican women are present in the most lucrative sex markets, many of them subject to forms of trafficking and debt servitude (US Department of State 2004). Activities involving the exploitation of prostitutes are temporally segmented, in unison with those who run the prostitution markets in the destination countries. Once the first contacts have been made and the machinery started up, once the business has been shown to be profitable, the attractive power of the 'rich' markets becomes the decisive factor in the reproduction of migratory flows of women for forced prostitution. The circuits are initially fortuitous and unstructured, and the passage is gradual from unorganized forms of exploitation to integrated commercial systems. We shall now look more closely at two modes of expansion. The first developed in Europe, along land routes from parts of Eastern Europe and eventually the ex-Soviet Central Asian republics; here there will be a special focus on the Albanian system. The second mode of expansion, which generally takes place 'to order', developed over very long distances, as in the case of the intercontinental traffic from Thailand and Russia to the United States and other rich parts of the world; here, we shall focus especially on the trafficking of Nigerian women to Europe.

Movements within Europe

It has been calculated that roughly a quarter of women subjected to sex exploitation in the world come from the countries of Central and Eastern Europe.[1] In 1997 the OSCE estimated that at least 175,000 young women, including minors, had been trafficked from that region to become prostitutes in Central and Western Europe; today the figure has grown, and the International Organization for Migration puts it at a minimum of 200,000 (Lehti 2003). The phenomenon first appeared following the collapse of the Soviet system: data on the forced prostitution of young women from East-Central Europe and even the Balkans tell us that their exploiters often invented the activity, with no prior experience in the field, and showed great resourcefulness in adapting to the market conditions they found in the destination countries. The first routes took shape after the fall of the Berlin Wall, the breakup of the Soviet Union and the Yugoslav crisis, within a broader migratory movement towards other European countries or overseas. The first women intended for forced prostitution were driven to move from East-Central Europe to countries in Western Europe, particularly those which were easier to cross into illegally. Veritable chains of clandestine migration, run by methods typical of human trafficking, took shape in the early 1990s in Austria and Germany, where Polish and Czech men began to organize the prostitution of Polish and Czech women in various low-category hotels. The exploiters were starting their business from scratch as they adapted to the varied conditions in local markets. During the same years the first Russian women were introduced illegally or with tourist visas to Finland, where rackets already existed for the exploitation of women from Southeast Asia; one study calculates that by 1998, 86.6 per cent of prostitutes trafficked to Greater Helsinki were Russian-speaking (OSCE 2002). Given that in Finland most prostitution is mobile in form, it seems that Russian men generally made Russian women sell sex in camper vans, or else continually moved them around from one hotel or motel to another. In Italy, the same period witnessed a spread of street prostitution, which was mainly run by Albanian men exploiting female compatriots and tending to draw in women from more distant countries.

In the 1990s, trafficking gradually extended into larger and larger areas. From countries of origin directly bordering the Schengen area (mainly Poland, the Czech Republic, Russia, Albania and Hungary), the recruiters spread mainly eastward to parts of the Balkans and all the former Soviet republics, eventually including those of Central Asia as well. At the same time, the women who arrived in Europe began to be moved further afield, to France, Belgium, the Netherlands, Spain and Britain. Since it was so easy to cross frontiers, it took only a few years for Italy, Finland,

Germany and Austria to become transit zones (US Department of State 2000) and catchment areas for trafficked women, who were then passed on to other countries of the EU. As the areas of destination, origin and transit grew ever larger, the routes themselves gradually became longer and more structured.

The places driving this movement were those in which the greatest profits could be made. At first, the parts of Europe where the prostitution market offered the greatest potential were the main urban centres of the 'historic' countries of the European Union. Over the next fifteen years, however, the centres of attraction for traffickers have become more numerous, three of them being especially profitable. The first area, on the margins of the EU, comprises the Czech Republic, Poland and the Baltic republics, which immediately after the collapse of the Soviet bloc became flooded with money-bearing Western sex tourists. The flow of German clients remains steady, so that in Cheb, for example, a tourist town in the Czech Republic with 32,000 inhabitants, it is estimated that at least 10,000 Germans arrive each weekend to purchase consumption goods and the cut-price sex services offered by women from Eastern Europe (UNODC 2004a). The Baltic states are another favourite destination for visitors from northern Europe, while by the mid-1990s Hungary already had an international reputation as a centre of sex tourism much coveted by international traffickers and exploiters. In some parts of the Balkans – Kosovo and Bosnia-Herzegovina, in particular – it was the large-scale presence of foreign military contingents and international peacekeepers which rapidly created a high demand for prostitution in the 1990s; local criminal organizations knew how to seize the opportunity, obviously at the expense of thousands of young women and girls.[2] A more recent trend has been the expansion of sex markets in countries further inland, such as Bulgaria, Moldova and Romania, and in the Balkans as a whole this

Sex Traffic

spread has been especially marked in the last two to three years. Originally involved as lands of origin for prostitution markets, this area has started to be combed by recruiters and transporters capable of building their own exploitation networks. But it should be stressed that in many of these countries the organization of flows of women 'for export' long preceded the birth of local forms of exploitation. Indeed, more generally, in many ex-Communist countries it was precisely the trafficking in women that sustained the development of local prostitution markets. The markets there are highly profitable because they are based on intensive forms of exploitation: international organizations estimate, for example, that in the Balkans 90 per cent of foreign women engaged in prostitution, both adults and minors, have been victims of trafficking (UNICEF 2002). The markets where they are exploited have recently grown in both number and size, not least in countries that have recently joined the EU, and in Russia. In all these areas, the system tends to reproduce itself through the same principle of the division of labour, as the need asserts itself for a constant replenishment of cheap women from abroad. Exploitation on the spot, by criminal networks made up of both locals and foreigners, is fed by the ceaseless movement of women.

The first destinations, the countries of Western Europe, served as models for the development of this system; it was there that the traffickers learned to refine their trade, and to practise the most effective methods of exploitation, which were then taken over and imitated in the countries of origin and transit. To form a clear picture of long-term flows across Eurasia, most of it by land, we should imagine a cluster of movements which, with a few exceptions, take place from east to west and from south to north. The areas crossed may be distinguished as Set A, Set B and Set C, the last and most peripheral of these being exclusively an area of flows towards the other two. The zones of Set A, most of them within the Schengen area, constitute the principal markets: they are the richest destination countries, and perhaps also the countries of subsequent transit to other parts of Set A. The zones of Set B, which lie outside the EU or have only recently joined it, are destination areas for major flows from Set C, as well as areas of transit towards Set A. The zones in Set B may in turn be areas of origin for flows directed to zone A. It is important to note that the markets in area B are also used for the selection and grooming of the 'best' women for the markets of zone A; the competitive mechanisms triggered by the high number of girls in circulation ensure that only those likely to be most profitable are chosen to continue the journey westward. It follows that, although Western Europe is the zone where the early forms of exploitation established themselves, Central and Eastern Europe is the region that sees the most trafficking today. Associations working in that region to assist young women and girls have reported cases where they are so disoriented that they are no longer able to tell which country they are in (Butterwek 1999).

Within the vast area of Central and Eastern Europe, the flows rapidly change direction. In general, the routes tend to stretch further and further east: commercial sex circuits may now start in Tajikistan – where local women are sold abroad for between $2,000 and $7,000 (IOM 2001f) – and end in Russia or the Middle East. Nowadays the former Soviet Asian republics mainly stand out as areas of recruitment; the international organizations and NGOs report a growing number of cases of trafficking in the Caucasus, where interregional trafficking is also now said to be widespread (Aslanov 2002). The migration of young women, mostly duped about the nature of the work in store for them abroad, has begun in Armenia and Georgia – countries where emigrants, most of them without proper documents, account for 1 million out of 5 million inhabitants – and Azerbaijan, Tajikistan,

Kazakhstan (where 2 million out of a population of 15 million are emigrants) and the Kirghiz Republic. The trafficking has given rise to forms of polarization, as Kazakhstan and Kirghizstan have become transit areas for women coming from Uzbekistan and Tajikistan. Already in 1999, at least 4,000 women left the Kirghiz Republic for various destinations – one-third for Central Europe, two-thirds for Western Europe, China and the Middle East – and the flows have been rising at a dizzying pace.[3] US agencies report that Uzbekistan, Kazakhstan and Ukraine are the three countries recently under greatest pressure from recruiters – a pressure about to exceed even that on Moldova (US Department of State 2004).

From country of origin to country of transit: Moldova

Two distinct periods may be identified in the evolution of trafficking in the European region. The first was the one in which early groups of organized traffickers successfully entered the Schengen area, while also retaining solid contacts that allowed them to restock in their hinge countries of origin: Poland, Czech Republic, Hungary and Lithuania, as well as the former Yugoslavia and Albania. Gradually recruiters from these countries managed to bring about a knock-on effect, in the form of female migratory flows from neighbouring regions. To some extent they also obstructed passing migration: as we shall see, young women without documents who headed for Albania, in the hope of entering Italy or Greece, invariably ended up in the hands of traffickers. In general, the hinge countries have become places for the catchment and grooming of girls from further east, who are then sent to markets in the West waiting to receive them. Over time, the recruitment areas tend to become larger and more diverse. Thus, in 1999 the great majority of women in transit to the Czech Republic and

Poland – a country with at least 15,000 new arrivals each year – were still coming from the former Soviet republics, but there was already a growing number who had originated in the Balkans (Bulgaria and Romania).

The second period in the evolution of trafficking began in the late 1990s, when the easternmost areas of Europe and the Balkans (which had previously been areas of origin) also became important areas of transit and exploitation, with highly organized forms of trafficking. Today, for example, Romania and Bulgaria form, together with Serbia, the main areas through which women pass on their way from the former Soviet republics to the West. Since the route through Albania has been effectively closed (Monzini, Pastore and Sciortino 2003), and since only a tourist visa is now required to travel from Bulgaria and Romania to the EU, the latter two countries have become the favoured hub for the trafficking of Ukrainian and Moldovan women, as well as women from Belarus, Uzbekistan, the Baltic republics and even the Balkans: so much so that recently even Albanian and Macedonian groups stock up on women there (Transcrime 2003: 45; US Department of State 2004). For traffickers always choose the roads with the fewest bumps, where official checks are the least efficient and the most shaped by the workings of corruption.

Moldova presents an interesting example of the gradual change from a country of origin to a country of transit. Since the early 1990s, thousands of girls have left this tiny country each year for Western Europe, Israel and the Balkans; it has been calculated that in the year 2000 alone at least 10,000 girls aged between 15 and 22 set off on these routes, without any kind of guarantee. According to the most recent research, the girls who are recruited are very often minors, and most of them belong to the Turkish minority; many too are young mothers (OSCE 2003). The most heavily used routes to Europe pass through Hungary, Slovenia or the Balkan countries. In previous years, thousands of girls went as far as Albania, before moving back up to Italy and Western Europe. Today women tend to use other routes, running up a debt of perhaps $1,500 in exchange for a three-month tourist visa and a ride in a coach or car with various companions. The costs fall if the traffickers cross frontiers illegally. But, in any event, a girl ends up owing her trafficker at least $5,000 by the time she is sold on the European markets.

Despite the increased number of police checks and forced repatriations to Moldova, the business is still highly profitable – as we can see from the fact that recruiters pick through the remotest villages, which sometimes lack everything, even electricity, and where it is still easy to operate through trickery. The age range of the enlisted women has grown wider, as has the gamut of destination countries. It would appear, for example, that women over 30 who are formally recruited as home helps or babysitters are mostly destined for Turkish markets, whereas young girls are mostly sent to Russia (IOM 2004). In accordance with the EU policy of repatriating women who have no valid documents, the routes out of Moldova have changed and since 2003 increasingly end elsewhere (US Department of State 2004). The new destinations – especially Turkey, Russia and the Gulf States – make it an excellent investment, given that there is virtually no chance for the girls to return and the local authorities offer them no assistance. The new currents have therefore become more diverse than before: on the one hand, a dual flow towards Turkey and Russia, where the illegal trip costs $100 and $500 respectively (IOM 2004: 93); on the other hand, a highly lucrative flow to the Gulf States, where the outlay on air travel is greater but so are the profits for the exploiters.

Much slicker groups have therefore established themselves alongside the small, cash-strapped organizations that operate with amateurish false documents or specialize in illegal frontier-crossings. These new rackets are capable of moving groups of women from country to country by legal methods, with the help of other subgroups and individuals; the ease of forging papers, together with high-level corruption and scant border controls, have increased the capacity to organize trips over a long distance. In Moldova, apparently, a passport can be put together in a couple of hours, while no more than a couple of days are needed for other documents (IOM 2004: 104–5). The package deal for a girl consists of a passport, an entry permit, and a visa for tourism or work in the entertainment industry. Since the process is costly and requires an investment with high returns, most of the girls – who will go to work in bars or nightclubs – are trained in a series of stages. In Chisinau, the capital of Moldova, some nightclubs have been identified which operate as preparation centres for as many as fifty girls at a time, Moldovan but also Romanian, Russian and Ukrainian, who are taught to dance and to serve customers. Groups of local as well as Russian, Lebanese, Syrian and Egyptian traffickers make use of this service. The training lasts a couple of months in all, during which the girls are treated gently. The assessment takes place during the first month and a decision is made about their destination; then they are taught how to bargain with customers, how to demand payment for extra services, and so on. Finally they are sent abroad, to Lebanon, the United Arab Emirates and above all Russia, with proper documents and the complicity of the local embassy. Some continuity of operations is assured through well-structured protection rackets involving the public authorities, police officers, embassy staff and politicians. Investigators have found that it is difficult to intercept this kind of trafficking, which is often invisible and leads to extreme forms of exploitation; only the direct testimony of victims has, on occasion, brought its existence to light (IOM 2004).

Mechanisms in other parts of the world

We have now seen that the European flows originate and expand in accordance with a principle of geographical progression. In Europe itself, they grow in parallel with the new centres for the trafficking and exploitation of women, while over the past fifteen years the organization of trafficking in the Eurasian area has gone together with a marked rise in the overall level of prostitution. The same mechanism has manifested itself in other parts of the world: Bangkok became a magnet attracting flows from Vietnam, China, Cambodia and Indonesia, flows which then expanded in all directions throughout the region (Southeast Asia Watch 1998). In the subcontinent, India is the main destination for women coming from Nepal and Bangladesh, but another flow heads out from India to the Middle East (Ahmad 2001). In the case of Africa, South Africa and Nigeria have provided the main force of attraction (Sita 2003), while in Latin America the flows are highly complex and undergoing expansion (Bibes 2001).

All over the world, land trafficking – which does not require large investment – usually involves an ongoing buying and selling of women, and leads to sometimes quite tortuous journeys. Some trafficking supplies markets that are not very profitable. Conversely, long-distance routes require complex organization and are geared only to the richest markets, especially those of the great Western and Asian metropolises. Those who plan the trips have to be capable of acting at two levels: they must both coordinate the transport and guarantee a secure system of exploitation. Generally the two are organized separately, by people with special areas of competence, and in each phase an initial investment of capital is required. For the transport, apart from the cost of flights, it is necessary to find reliable guides for the girls at each stage, to grease the palms of well-placed bureaucrats, and to pay for the services of forgers. For the exploitation, it is necessary to find living accommodation, to organize the women's daily lives, and to ensure that there is a secure place, indoors or outdoors, where they can be prostituted. Organizers with good protection and enough money for investment will get a better return: the more they spend on a place for prostitution, the more they can charge clients and the higher will be their income.

On long trips, the investment of money and time is high both for the traffickers and for the women; the initial agreement between them is therefore usually put in writing, or anyway precisely defined, although that does not mean that it is not later disregarded. Unlike in the Balkans or Eastern Europe, the system used to keep a hold on women over long distances relies not so much on blackmail or physical violence as on the size of the debt and the impossibility of returning to the woman's home country. What links the system of land travel and geographical progression with the long-distance system is that each new route is operated by criminal gangs and networks that gradually specialize in travel or exploitation. In this way, the flows can be spread more widely into new destination areas, and more and more countries of origin can be added to the list.

The land routes

The Albanian system

Albanian officials estimate that at least 30,000 of their female compatriots are exploited as prostitutes in Western and Eastern Europe, and that they are now found all over the continent, from Poland to Norway. Thousands are minors, with a majority aged between 13 and 25.[4] Their migratory flow began in 1991 and has the peculiarity that each of the girls leaves in the company of an ethnically Albanian exploiter. In fact, at least in the early period, the business often took the form of emigration *à deux* to Italy. Once there, at first sporadically, then in ever more structured forms, the Albanian pimps put their girls on the streets to serve local customers. The lack of official prevention strategies, and the high level of customer interest in such young girls, encouraged growing numbers of Albanians to follow in their wake; many girls were indeed eager to leave, though mostly quite unaware of what awaited them. New or aspiring pimps who lacked any experience saw the prospect of making a lot of money with very few risks.

In the early years, at least, it cannot have been easy for Albanian men to exploit women in this way, if only because it conflicts with the usual code of honour in their society and with some of the values typical of Mediterranean 'masculinity'. On the other hand, the whole apparatus of violence used to persuade women to work as regular prostitutes – an apparatus involving threats, beating, burning, blows on the back and ice-cold showers in the middle of the night – seems to be at least in part culturally acceptable by virtue of the subaltern role of women. Pimping is based on a close and ambiguous male–female relationship, which includes physical violence and is psychologically and socially facilitated by the woman's subject position. It is an old model in which the man, who is in a relationship with the woman, accompanies her to work and then spends the day in a bar, together with male friends in the same racket. He shares certain interests with them – often illegal business of another kind, such as the buying and selling of drugs. Every now and then, he and his friends take it in turns to check up on their women walking different sections of the street; or else they ring them on their mobile to make sure everything is going well. Sometimes they take them to a restaurant, where everyone celebrates a birthday or anniversary together.

This schema spread in the early 1990s to Italy, especially the wealthier regions in the North, and developed into a much more professional, and rational, system of exploitation. It is a system hard to bear for the women, and much more lucrative for the exploiters. As soon as they see a chance, the latter bring over their own male relatives – brothers, cousins, brothers-in-law – who arrive with girls in tow and start up the same kind of activity. Gradually, the formation of solid chains makes it possible to expand the business, increasing the number of girls exploited by each man. For this reason the growth of demand in Albania leads to the rise of specialized recruiters. The buying of girls then begins in earnest, usually two or three per pimp, either Albanian or from parts of the former Soviet Union and the Balkans.

Let us take the case of one Albanian youngster from Kosovo:

> She was trafficked when she and her family were living in a refugee camp in Albania. She was only 13 years old. She met an 18-year-old man who offered to marry her and she ran away with him. He then sent her to Italy where she was forced into prostitution for three years. Later he took her to Holland where he also forced her into prostitution, before returning to Italy. During all these years, she was severely beaten and abused. She has had two abortions and both her arms were broken. The trafficker and his [real] wife were watching her every move and even followed her when she was driven away by clients. Finally she was deported from Italy to Albania when she was caught with a false passport. From Albania, she was repatriated to Kosovo by IOM and reunited with her family. She did not dare to tell her family what had happened to her and told them that she had married and lived with the man. He called several times a day threatening to kill her if she did not return to Italy. Her family was very worried but also were unaware of the conditions she could expect. She returned to Italy after one week in Kosovo. (IOM 2004: 66)

The mechanism of exploitation usually means that the first woman launched into prostitution – if she proves capable and is not replaced as a lover – will continue to work for her man but step up a grade, perhaps assuming a function in the supervision of other girls. In addition to streetwalking herself, her responsibilities might then include the collection of her colleagues' daily earnings, bookkeeping, household budgeting, and general provision for unforeseen circumstances that might affect the group. If her pimp is temporarily arrested, she will make up parcels to take to prison, collect money for a lawyer, and handle everything else as best she can. Her subordinates, on the other hand, are forced into exhausting work rhythms to repay the debt to the pimp they incurred at the moment of purchase. Once they are bound by this debt system, they are deprived of their passport, placed within an established network of lodgings, assigned to a precise section of the street, accompanied, escorted and threatened. The boss's woman keeps constant watch over them.

Girls who enter the group in this subaltern role may have been recruited in Albania, by trickery or violence, according to the methods we have already mentioned; or – especially if they are not of Albanian origin – they may have been bought on the Albanian or Italian market. In Italy, the price in 1999 for a girl with a passport who had already been 'educated' could be around 6 million lire, or less than $3,000: this included a three-month 'surety', in the sense that the traffickers undertook to supply a replacement if she escaped during that period.[5] These mechanisms for the expansion of trafficking are reflected in a conversation between two Albanian pimps – let us call them Lorenc and Skender – whom the police intercepted in a town in central Italy. Skender spoke of how well things had gone for him in France, where girls 'work all hours and earn more', and warmly advised Lorenc to try his luck across the Alps. Lorenc, who was looking for a girl to buy cheap, asked Skender whether he knew of a 'good deal'. Skender replied that the only one he knew of was a gypsy, because at the moment Albanian girls were in short supply. Lorenc then asked Skender, who was about to leave for Albania, whether he could personally find a new girl for him. Skender did not think this was a good idea, and said it was much better to buy foreign girls. Lorenc did in fact soon buy a Romanian girl, using a network of Albanian intermediaries who operated in his part of Italy.[6]

Delivery of women from the Balkans

Albanian girls were recruited first in the towns, then more and more in poor, remote areas of north-east Albania, especially the districts of Mat, Diber and Peshkopi. Here the phenomenon has become truly alarming: in some parts of the interior, which re-cruiters have combed on a massive scale, families are so afraid of seeing their daughters disappear that they have stopped sending them to school (Renton 2001). Girls are recruited very young, and in fact 80 per cent of those who have returned to Albania, and received assistance, said they were minors when they began to work as prostitutes (IOM 2004a: 23). In the late 1990s, when the supply of Albanian girls was drying up, the prostitution rackets turned to girls arriving in Albania on the 'Balkan trail', since by then the Balkan Peninsula had become a major transit route for persons leaving Romania, Moldova, Ukraine and Russia. It was a very long and complicated route, picking up women all along the way, from Russia via Ukraine, Moldova and Romania, and also Hungary, then through Serbia and Montenegro (always a key stage) and on to Albania. Many of the women remained in the Balkans, especially Kosovo and Bosnia, but the majority made it to Albania and then, with the help of smugglers' dinghies, continued their journey to Italy and other European countries. This has become a firmly established route, despite its tortuous and geographically absurd composition. For, first of all, Albanian gangs are a major player in the illegal traffic from Eastern Europe to Italy and the West: not only illegal immigration and the smuggling of cocaine, heroin, marijuana and weapons, but also trafficking in women for the Western prostitution markets. Second, the whole of the Balkans offers ideal conditions for this business: that is, an acute social and economic malaise, solidly rooted criminal gangs, and fragmentation into a number of micro-states whose police forces are riddled with corruption and not given to regular cooperation with one another.

While traffickers find excellent opportunities in the Balkans, the consequences for women are appalling. Those who cross the region to enter Western Europe, as well as those who set out intending to work in the prostitution markets, are very likely to be subjected to traumas and acts of violence, ranging from forced confinement to physical brutality, and to receive threats of death to themselves or their family. As we know from evidence given to the police and courts in Italy, women who ventured into this region in the late 1990s were very lucky to reach Italy and the EU unscathed. One Romanian woman, already expelled once from Italy and forced to emigrate again for serious family reasons, stated that she had 'promised herself' never 'to make the same mistake as before'. However, although she knew the ropes, when she arrived in Albania she was again bought, isolated and beaten, threatened with death and violence to her family. But this time she decided to report her exploiters to the police once she got to Italy (Tribunale di Lecce 2001b).

From the women's point of view, the first part of the journey – from Ukraine to Belgrade – does not usually involve major problems, since traffickers have no need to use violence in their work. Recruited by acquaintances or agencies, which have usually obtained their exit papers and organized the first stage of the trip, the women have no intention of breaking off the journey and are unaware of what awaits them. They travel in small groups, accompanied for short stretches by intermediaries of various nationalities. Each intermediary takes delivery by handing over a sum of money to the one before him, then completes his stretch and sells the girls on at a higher price to the next link in the chain, usually after the crossing of a frontier. Although there are some cases of a non-stop journey by coach, this kind of 'combination route' seems to be the one most widely used to reach the Serbian capital.[7] Belgrade, the real gateway to the Balkans, has become a hub for traffic heading towards Slovenia and Albania, from where it is possible to gain access to the Schengen area. In this city are the places where women without documents are most frequently turned into commodities, to be placed on the cheap markets for commercial sex; it was the launching pad for the human auctions, or sales, which have since spread to other Balkan capitals and frontier zones. After Belgrade, the women are taken either to Kosovo and Bosnia or to Montenegro and Albania. The property can here change hands several times, so that the girls may spend weeks, or months, moving from one owner to another. After each handover, someone takes them by car to a private room, in the country or the city, where they are kept in isolation. One day the time comes – usually in Albania, but sometimes in the former Yugoslavia – when the women must be persuaded to bow to the fate in store for them, often by means of brutal violence, with repeated rapes, or gang rapes, mixed in with beatings. It seems to be a common practice to film or photograph the girls while they are suffering the worst violence, so that the pictures can later be used to blackmail them with the threat of sending a copy to their family back home. The systems used for the handover of women at this point are different, in both form and substance, from those used in the previous phase. Even if the basis is always an act of selling, the purchasers this time have to make a selection: they look at the women well before paying up, and they touch them – for the next handover will probably be to people who work in the front line of the prostitution racket. Here, before choosing, there has to be a careful valuation based on full knowledge of the facts. Such buying and selling often go together with forms of physical and psychological violence.

The sale may take place in the open air, or in a hotel, garage or apartment, and it may closely resemble a real auction. The women are sold, at various prices, with or without a passport – although the document itself will not be in their possession but have been exchanged between one trafficker and another. The prices are based on the length of the journey, the woman's age, beauty and bearing, her character and her presumed capacity for adaptation.

The system of basing the price of each girl on supply and demand is very advantageous to the traffickers: it allows them to extract the maximum from her, and at the same time affects her psychologically by inducing a sure sense of debasement and alienation. The knowledge that she is being sold, in front of other persons, ensures that she will be easier to manage. This handover marks her entry into a circuit where the act of exchange may take place over and over again,[8] and where a constant threat is present at each 'resale'. It is a depraved mechanism, because each 'transfer of ownership' automatically increases the girl's price and, with it, her personal debt to the exploiter who buys her. Since the basic rule is that each girl must 'repay' her owner the price he paid for her, she finds that this price keeps being doubled, tripled or quadrupled; the investment has to bear the maximum yield.

At each handover, the girl suffers violence even if she behaves 'well', for she must learn again who is boss, who has command over her. To prevent her from escaping, each new trafficker has to reinforce her subjugation and demonstrate his own strength. The system used to break her will is so harsh that, once the girl reaches her destination and is set to work, she will often say that it seems like the end of a nightmare; some recall Albania with real terror and feel that the worst part of their experience is behind them. Nevertheless, the same system of selling that they endured in the Balkans may be repeated in the destination countries: cases have been recorded, for example, at the motorway grill near the border with Slovenia, and in Puglia, shortly after the sea crossing from Albania to Italy (Carroll 2000).

The final act of sale, whatever the form and place in which it occurs, fixes the sum that the woman will have to pay back to her owner. Once she reaches her destination, she must start working to liquidate the debt: that is, the money paid to purchase her, plus the cost of the false documents that the owner had to obtain for her, plus the (multiplied) cost of her own keep. These subjugation techniques that underpin the relationship of exploitation have gradually spread beyond the original Albania–Italy axis. In the last few years, the Albanian networks have taken hold in more and more parts of Western Europe, always with the same basic features. Everywhere criminal gangs, based on tight clan and family relations or a common local background, have developed a remarkable capacity to adapt and root themselves in a new environment. In Belgium, the Netherlands and Germany, they have come to occupy large shares of the underground markets, bringing with them girls who work for a very low price; indeed, prostitutes controlled by Albanian gangs are now competitive even on the Czech and Polish markets. Recently, since the closure of the irregular sea frontier with Puglia, the routes into Western Europe have changed. More and more Albanian girls are being deported from Greece, Belgium, Holland, the UK, France, Germany and Norway, whereas the total number of repatriations from Italy is falling. The less organized trafficking still involves false papers and illegal crossing of frontiers – for example, across the mountains into Greece, or over tortuous land routes. But police report that today's better-organized Albanian traffickers mostly operate 'clean' systems, in which girls travel by air with false papers and are able to rely on the complicity of frontier officials. They land at an airport in the destination country, sometimes after catching another plane in a different Balkan country. In general, all the countries that have seen a rise in organized crime networks from Eastern Europe and the Balkans also stress the frontline role of Albanians in the prostitution and drugs rackets; the British authorities, for instance, report considerable problems from Albanian gangs, especially in the London area (Home Office 2004). According to Transcrime (2003), Albanians have used many of the contacts they developed through the drugs traffic to help organize markets in forced prostitution.

Albanians have managed to establish themselves in all countries by building a strong network of mutual support (IOM 2004). In the exploitation of prostitution, the system of small groups operating indoors or outdoors always involves tight control over the women, day and night. They move frequently around the host country, and in the event of danger are capable of disappearing very quickly. They instil the women with a deep sense of social isolation, both by underlining the climate of xenophobia in the host country, and by showing off their relations with the local police. In France and Belgium, as well as in London, it has been observed that the most intricate trafficking systems are run by Albanians, and it is difficult for girls to denounce their own exploiters (OSCE 2002; Europol 2004).

Intercontinental trafficking

The organization of Russian traffickers

In Russia and Ukraine, the trafficking of women for exploitation as prostitutes began in the early 1990s and soon spread to all continents. Some Russian and Ukrainian groups with enough capital, and the necessary organizational abilities, launched highly sophisticated businesses right from the start, taking advantage of modern technologies such as the Internet to find girls and advertise for clients in search of 'escorts'. In the case of women offering their services voluntarily, a 'seasonal' contract specified every conceivable detail before departure, although the terms were not respected once they were abroad; the contracts might be for work as home helps, babysitters or au pairs, or else as 'entertainers'. Unlike other groups – Albanian, Nigerian or Polish, for example – which put together their own underground networks, Russian traffickers soon developed a capacity to disguise their business behind legally recognized employment, travel or marriage agencies. Given the widespread use of the Russian language among the whole of the ex-Soviet peoples, these organizations rich in capital, entrepreneurship and market strategies gradually managed to bring the most profitable part of the business under their control (the part originating in Eastern Europe), and to dominate lucrative markets halfway round the world, where women from the former USSR were highly appreciated. The agencies attracted and selected the 'best' girls from the vast area of Russia and its neighbours, provided them with documents and tourist visas, accompanied them to the airport, and handed them over to people whose job it was to accompany them to their final destination. Women were also recruited from the structured local prostitution scene, which had a high percentage of minors. According to current estimates, St Petersburg has between two and four hundred private agencies offering sexual services at home (ECPAT 2003); and official statistics speak of 100,000 prostitutes in Moscow alone, 70 per cent of them victims of trafficking from former Soviet republics and other parts of Russia, and more than 80 per cent under age (IOM 2004b).

The most tightly organized groups arrange the employment of girls abroad through semi-clandestine structures, usually day or night clubs but also escort agencies; these enable them to control as many as one hundred women each, in the world's most structured sex markets. The documents allowing trouble-free travel are obtained through corruption both at home and abroad, in frontier posts and embassies. The women themselves, cheated about the work in store for them, are saddled with huge debts or handed over to violent exploiters capable of forcing them to obey. The reputation of Russians as 'tops' in the criminal world helps them to make agreements with the most powerful criminal organizations, such as the Japanese yakuza or groups in the Balkans and Turkey. These structured networks of accomplices make it easier for them to conduct successful business over long distances: at least 4,000 women arrive each year in the USA from Russia, and thousands more rotate among Bangkok, Hong Kong, Beijing, Singapore, Japan, the Middle East, Israel and Turkey (O'Neill-Richard 2000). In these countries women are slotted into existing rackets, which may be run on slavery-like lines or with systems that the women find more tolerable. The treatment is harshest in the United Arab Emirates, where prostitutes are exploited in apartments which they are not allowed to leave. Often, however, it is difficult to draw the dividing line between different degrees of exploitation: the worst can be found not only in the low-price sectors of the market (which involve long hours and a large throughput of clients) but also in the most expensive clubs (whose women have run up large debts from their journey and usually do not have papers in order). Even women with a regular job contract – such as ballerinas or entertainers – often have no control over their working conditions and no freedom of movement, living as they do without documents and under constant threat of blackmail. But it is more difficult for them to think of themselves as victims, even if they are forced to perform services against their will. Moreover, in the rare event of a police investigation, it is easier for the owner to say that he is not aware of any prostitution activity (IOM 2004a: 56).

The United States and Canada are among the main destinations for this kind of trafficking: once the women arrive there, they may discover that they have to repay debts as high as $15,000 (Protection Project 2002a). In the United States, where Russian women live in closed immigrant communities, socially isolated and stigmatized because of their occupation, they are mistrustful of the authorities and unlikely to denounce their exploiters. The women run by Russian or Ukrainian groups actually come from various countries of Eastern Europe, and work in saunas, massage parlours, bars or apartments. To avoid checks, their controllers rent a number of apartments and send along clients who contact them by telephone; most of the places in question are under repair and available for six to twelve months, at a price of a few thousand dollars (Gomez 2001: 34). There is a system of rotation from one place to another, especially after police raids. As in Europe, women also move around a lot between or within states (Gomez 2001: 54), but the regional or local routes vary considerably in length. In the northeast, the evidence points to flows among Massachusetts, Delaware and Washington, and between Rhode Island and Georgia. Thai women, on the other hand, are shunted from the Arizona or Texas border country up to Massachusetts. New York is a major centre of exploitation, as well as of transit towards New Jersey, Pennsylvania, Florida, California, and Washington.

For the girls, the trips are long and tortuous. One 15-year-old Ukrainian, for instance, who was found in wretched circumstances in Seattle, had first been recruited in her village and sent to the Ukrainian capital, Kiev. From there she was moved to St Petersburg and by train to Moscow, then put on a plane for Germany, another train from Frankfurt to Paris, and a transatlantic flight to

Montreal. She then spent several weeks travelling by car or mini-van through Canada to Vancouver, and ended up being exploited in Portland and Seattle. Since she had no proper papers, the people organizing her trip avoided the frontier between Canada and the United States, which she crossed on foot together with three other girls and their traffickers (Estes and Weiner 2001: 137). The switching process is much faster within individual cities: it has been noted in New Jersey, for example, that thousands of Russian women are frequently moved around between various bars and strip clubs. The market has a high capacity for investment and offers a good rate of return. Moreover, according to police reports, in the northeast, New York, the southeast and San Francisco, more than 70 per cent of the prostitution market is controlled, financed or at least supported by criminal groups of various origins. These groups are active not only in the big cities, and they are very skilful at organizing activity on a temporary, short-term basis. In-depth investigations suggest that most trafficking organizations have no more than five members, although there are also medium-sized ones (6–15 persons) and some very large ones indeed (50–100 persons) (Gomez 2001: 9–58). O'Neill-Richard (2000), whose research is based on interviews and other individual evidence, maintains that the business is in the hands not of big syndicates but of individuals and small groups in contact with one another, all of whom rely on the support of corrupt officials.

Israel is another major destination for women from Russia. According to a number of sources, Russian criminals have managed in the space of a few years to gain control over prostitution-related trafficking, once again thanks to important corrupt contacts inside the host country. The links between exploiters and policemen, who are often regular customers of brothels, are evident enough. It is certainly a lucrative business: women are sold for $5,000–10,000, and the government puts turnover related to prostitution at more than $400,000 (Hughes 2002). According to Israeli police estimates, there are between 1,000 and 3,000 trafficked women in the country, but NGOs argue that this refers only to annual flows and that the real figure is considerably higher. It is difficult to be sure of the scale of the problem, since the girls may be exploited in visible brothels, through an 'escort service' system or in highly discreet establishments. Many of the women deported between 2000 and 2002 were Russian, Ukrainian or Moldovan, and 78 per cent of their exploiters were Jews of Russian origin. Recently the number of women arriving from Moldova has been on the decline, while the component of women from Uzbekistan has been on the rise. The routes have traditionally passed through Moscow, but due to the tightening of airport controls the largest flow of women has moved through the Sinai desert, with the help of Bedouin groups. It is very difficult to cross the frontier. One woman reports:

> We were arranged in an Indian file, one after the other. They counted us, like you count sheep. Later I found out why. They got a thousand dollars for every girl who got through. We walked like that for half an hour, once we sat down, once we ran, once they told us to lie down. It was March and the sand was cold. We came to a barbed wire fence and they told us to climb it. A jeep came by on the other side and they told us to get in. But the jeep didn't stop. We had to jump into it as it was moving. They covered us with a tarpaulin and there was no air. Some of the girls passed out.

A common practice in Israel are auctions, at which women are displayed naked to would-be purchasers. As to the forms of exploitation, these can be quite varied. One woman, who was bought by a man in Nazareth, recalls:

> He used to arrange about 25 customers per day. I had to prepare food for him, his favourite food; he'd shout at me and beat me: 'It doesn't matter how many customers you've had today, I'll always be

your last customer.' He came to my room every night and raped me.
He loved hearing me screaming with pain. (Levenkron and Dahan
2003: 24)

The flow from Thailand

According to some estimates (O'Neill-Richard 1999), a third of
global trafficking in women and children takes place in or from
Southeast Asia. Outside the region, Japan, the United States,
Australia and certain West European countries are the most
frequent destinations for women of Thai origin who work as
prostitutes: there are thought to be at least 100,000 to 200,000,
with 50,000–70,000 in Japan alone (Protection Project 2002b).
These flows began to rise sharply in the 1980s. As things stand
today, although the work sometimes allows a degree of autonomy
and personal fulfilment, numerous circuits are controlled by exploiters who force the women to work at a slave-like pace. Often
Thai women organize the racket together with local partners,
adopting a highly profitable system of integrated exploitation.
Thus, a woman may be ordered in advance, flown in on a visa to
work in the entertainment industry and immediately assigned to
a particular massage parlour or brothel, whose owner confiscates
her passport and forces her to obey whatever rules he dictates.
The worldwide system of debt-based control operates almost
exclusively in closed premises. In Japan, it was fully developed
in the early 1980s through agreements between club owners and
so-called *mama-san*, the Thai women who organized the trip and
the exploitation. Initially, some 90 per cent of Thai girls in this
sector worked in conditions of semi-slavery, but things improved
in the 1990s and now the figure is thought to be around 20 per
cent. Prostitution work has become a sought-after activity in Japan:
even when they keep only the tips for themselves, women can
earn what would be a considerable amount in Thailand. Yet their

living and working conditions are undoubtedly oppressive. The rotation system, whereby women are passed to different groups or between different clubs and towns, adds up to a strong network of communication and exchange between managers and suppliers (Cameron and Newman 2004). As elsewhere, exploitation is based on debts and the difficulty of repaying them; three to four months is the least it takes. One woman who managed to clear her debt in eight months recalls: 'I had calculated that I must have paid it back long ago, but the (bar manager) kept lying to me and said she didn't have the same records as I did. During these eight months, I had to take every client that wanted me and had to work every day, even during my period' (Human Rights Watch 2000a). Despite the abuses, however, the girls feel too threatened to try to run away: their greatest fear is of being captured by the *yakuza* and sold to another establishment, since this would mean that their debt would be doubled (Phongpaichit et al. 1998: 167). It often happens that a woman who finally manages to pay off her debt and start working for herself is reported by her exploiters as an illegal immigrant, and deported.

A similar system of exploitation is prevalent in Europe. A woman working under it in Germany, for instance, earns 2.5 per cent of what customers pay for her services (Phongpaichit et al. 1998). In Britain, following recent investigations into a ring supplying Thai women to a number of brothels, a Horsley police operation revealed that three Thai exploiters had purchased women for £6,000 each, with the intention of making them work to pay off a debt more than three times larger (£22,000). It must be the case in every country that the yield from each woman is at least three times greater than the sum paid for her, so that, as various interviewees have reported, the only solution is to serve a large number of customers in as short a time as possible (Home Office 2004: 77). Numerous news reports have also highlighted the exploitation of Thai women in the United States, many of whom are bought in Thai markets and resold. In this way, they can end up with a debt as high as $40,000 (Protection Project 2002b). The existence of rings that organize flights abroad and enlist corrupt officials also makes it easier for single individuals to enter the business. A study conducted in 1995, for example, revealed the activity of a German man who organized tourist trips to Thailand and, with the help of Thai traffickers, managed to combine this with sending girls to the United States. Once there, watched round the clock in a basement room with bars on the window, the girls had to pay $35,000 – or serve 400 customers – to regain their liberty (King 2004: 189).

Within the USA, the exploitation of Thai women is especially common in New York, Los Angeles, Seattle and San Diego. The brothels, run by Asian gangsters, are often located in Chinatown, and the women are moved around on average once every two months (Gomez 2001: 38). Research indicates that the system in the United States is especially harsh, because sometimes the debt is never cleared and the exploitative relationship can last for years in conditions of real slavery. According to government reports, women may at worst live in places of confinement where they have to work from eleven in the morning until four at night, without receiving anything other than tips. The prostitutes, who use alcohol and sometimes drugs, are required to work without a condom if the customer demands it (US Department of State 2004: 13–14). The situation is similar in Australia. Even women who know what work awaits them are subjected to brutal treatment to ensure their blind obedience, so that any capacity to contract on their part is overridden. Robbed of their (often false) passport, the Thai women may be shut up in brothels, or in houses run by *mama-san*, where they are forced to work every day of the week under constant surveillance. Here too the debt to be repaid may come to $30,000 – which translates into 900 customers to be served (US Department of State 2004: 9).

A complex system: the routes from Nigeria

The origins of trafficking

As in the Thai case, African women who prostitute themselves abroad make up only a fraction of the women exploited throughout the African continent. In keeping with a global trend, the commercial sex business in Africa has expanded considerably in the last two decades, especially in border areas where the most dynamic economies encounter the most impoverished. The trafficking of young girls and children from Mozambique and Angola to South Africa, for example, is at the root of a marked increase in child prostitution and the emergence of a porn video industry that exports all over the world. Africa is also the scene of highly organized human trafficking for the plantation and household labour markets. In the region on which we shall focus here, West Africa, it seems that the female emigration channels often issue into the commercial sex markets. For example, a good 75 per cent of a study sample of women who had emigrated from Ghana to Ivory Coast were engaged in prostitution in varying degrees of subjugation (Anarfi 1998). The exploitation of prostitutes is also highly organized within Nigeria, where it mainly involves girls who have migrated from rural areas to the cities.

In the late 1980s, Nigerian vice rings began to establish a presence on the European markets, bringing with them women mainly from Nigeria, but also from Ghana, Cameroon and nearby English-speaking countries. This international specialization of Nigeria, as a country of origin and transit for the launching of prostitutes, was made easier by the widespread presence of organized crime, which in the last two decades has managed to break into illegal markets in various parts of the world and to lay down firm roots abroad.[9] Probably some Nigerian women who had started out as prostitutes themselves saw a great opportunity to earn large sums from such activity, if it could be planned and organized on a larger scale, and in the late 1980s there were those (usually men) who looked to invest capital in this sector, in order to send young women abroad and insert them into vice rings. The activity of these initial investors – who were known as 'sponsors' and thought of as benefactors – must have given a strong impetus to female emigration, as it became a realistic possibility even for women without any means of their own. For the sponsors, a network of 'reliable' Nigerian women who specialized in the exploitation of prostitution, and would take charge of the organization of emigration, guaranteed an excellent rate of return on their investment.

This 'sponsored' emigration, often based on deception about the nature of the work available abroad, soon dominated the migratory chains that had been springing up independently. In 1990–91 a number of distinct, almost standardized patterns of female emigration took shape for the cheap sector of the market based on a fast pace of exploitation.

Turnover rose with the help of small organizations specializing in the exploitation of prostitution, which spread out into European society without encountering any major obstacles. These organizations found especially fertile soil in Italy, where in the late 1980s the cheap-rate prostitution of African women was a novelty that made a great impact on customers.[10] The flow of women there underwent a sharp rise in the early 1990s, until the market reached saturation point, and since then it has remained constant, although Italy is still the main destination country for Nigerian women. At the same time, the routes have extended to France, Belgium and the Netherlands, where many Nigerian gangs of exploiters use the same methods, though mostly in brothel-like premises and apartments. The whole circuit, driven by financial incentives from sponsors, has acquired clear-cut organizational features since the initial period. In Italy, the vice rings that exploit African women are entirely run by Nigerian women, because it is they who pioneered the whole business, adapted themselves to the context of street prostitution, and gained the necessary experience to run other women and girls in the most profitable manner. We have seen that, in the Thai and Russian system, women are left to fend for themselves once they have been sold for cash to the frontline exploiter. The Nigerian system is more complex, however, because those who buy the girls in Europe do not usually become their exclusive 'owners'; they must also answer financially to the people who paid out for the initial trip, and to the recruiter back home who is still in touch with the family.

The organizations in which wealthy Nigerian 'sponsors' decide to invest their money consist of pairs of madams, or 'Mamans Loa', who usually work in tandem and are sometimes sisters or close relatives. One of them remains in Nigeria to continue recruiting would-be migrants, to keep in touch with their families, and gradually to repay, with interest, the capital invested by the sponsor.[11] The other lives in Europe, where she controls the girls' daily lives and extracts the planned profits, including the money necessary to run the organization. The complexity of the organization itself varies with the size of the turnover, but in any event it has to pay a number of people to help with the work of the madams in the two countries.

At first, when the trafficking had just started, girls would leave Lagos airport and fly straight to Rome, Amsterdam or Paris, where they would be received by the 'Italian' madam or one of her accomplices. As frontier controls were stepped up, however, the routes became more complicated. Nowadays, intermediary groups of traffickers exist to handle nothing other than the long trip from Nigeria to Europe. It is a very important and delicate stage in the process, especially in the frequent cases when the migrant does not have proper papers; then it is necessary to enlist the services of a forger or corrupt official, as well as attending to the practical details of the trip to the final destination. The organizations that perform this role consist of Nigerian men and women who, for an agreed price, take charge of the duly instructed girls and deliver them safe and sound to their 'owners', the madams, in the destination country.

The stages of the journey

To explain how the trafficking of Nigerian women functions, let us look more closely at the stages involved.

Apart from Lagos, the main areas of origin of the young women are Edo and Delta, two of the thirty-six states that make up the Nigerian Federation. According to local estimates, these territorial bases – where the actually affected area is gradually expanding – were the homeland of 80 per cent of the African women trafficked in the rich sex markets of Western Europe: not only in Italy, but also in the Netherlands, Belgium and Spain, as well as Libya, Morocco, Saudi Arabia and Kenya (Olateru-Olagbegi 1999). Especially in Edo State and its capital, Benin City, Europe has become a much-coveted destination for young women and their families; indeed, local reports state that families often exert great pressure on daughters to leave and work abroad. In one very interesting article, which shows how the trafficking of young women for prostitution is seen in Nigeria itself (Ofuoku 1999), we read the following story:

> Emasuen is a fifteen-year-old girl from a family of five. Her father died in 1997. Her mother considered that sending her daughter

to Italy was the surest way out of the problem the family faced. But Emasuen refused. She would not 'do work' in Italy.... But the mother consoled her by painting a very rosy picture of how the family's life would soon change for the better, for just that single sacrifice. [When the girl continued to refuse], her mother tongue-lashed her and threw her out of the family home. Emasuen agonized over her mother's action. Reluctantly, she walked back to her hours later to say she was ready to do her bidding and go to Italy.

The mother then sold a patch of land and the family house, to raise some of the money for the 'sponsor', a businessman able to organize trips to Turin and Palermo. In this particular case there was no 'madam' figure in Nigeria, and in fact, before sending the girl off, the 'sponsor' kept her in his home for a month in Benin City, teaching her various sexual practices and getting her to do housework for free. Once in Italy, Emasuen told her family little about her life there: she telephoned from time to time, but only to say general things about herself. After nine months, however, the mother received a sizeable sum of money from the 'sponsor', which allowed her to improve considerably the quality of life for the whole family. She started the construction of a two-storey house, in an elegant part of Benin City, and bought a new patch of land. In the end, the family as a whole seemed to have obtained positive results from the twist of fate; the negative consequences fell entirely on the girl's shoulders. Stories of this kind have a profound impact on Nigerian society and smooth the way for the phenomenon to be reproduced, yet many people are aware that there is not always a happy ending. According to another source, a family sold their home to send the sister to Europe, but the girl brought nothing back after three years except for a terrible disease, which despite constant treatment is still ravaging her body.

Local reports state that nowadays 70 per cent of women who leave know that they will have to work in commercial sex markets. Deception was widely practised at first, but now it is clear which labour market will be accessible to young Nigerian women in Italy and Europe. Still, although it is true that a month's earnings in this sphere are the equivalent of ten years in a factory, the constant reproduction of trafficking is – as some NGOs emphasize[12] – made possible by the lack of information. For family members do not have a clear idea of the kind of exploitation that the girls will encounter. Even those who know when they leave that they will be working as prostitutes imagine that the environment in which they live will be very different.

The most important thing of which both the girls and their families are ignorant is the system of blackmail and psychological coercion underpinning the whole business. Those who return with a fortune, perhaps even continuing to work for the 'ring', prefer not to speak about such matters.

The most recent flows to Europe have mainly consisted of young women with an education that may have reached secondary school level but is often non-existent. The population of street prostitutes in Italy includes a growing number of women without any education, aged between 15 and 20. Most of them used to work in the Nigerian countryside, or in an insecure job as an employee or waitress on the outskirts of a large town, where the economic crisis threatened to leave them without pay for months at a time. They are usually young women for whom emigration seemed the only practicable solution. It is not difficult to recruit such people, given the crisis situation in Nigeria and the great power of attraction that a trip abroad exerts on their imagination.

Whereas the initial approach is easy, the stage of specifying the contract proves to be more complicated. The agreements in question, which are supposed to be up to the same standard as commercial transactions, are worked out in a number of meetings at which any disputes among the sponsors, madams and girls can be settled. The high degree of organization in the trafficking business is clear from the fact that, not only in Nigeria but also in Italy, special places are set aside for the administration of oaths, and that certain people with authority are given special powers to settle disputes and to ensure that the agreements are respected (Olateru-Olagbegi 1999: 7).

Before the women leave for Europe, they are offered a formal written contract, or else a verbal agreement supported by oaths and voodoo or 'juju' rituals. The system chosen depends on the social-cultural background of the women involved: those from villages in the interior, who are often illiterate and unable to pay anything up front, set great store by the spoken word and are required to swear an oath before the village elder or the 'sponsor' or the madam, who thereby assumes the role of middleman and guarantor to the 'sponsor' who advances the money. In this way, the oath becomes a basic element of subjugation for the girl and her family. A written contract, on the other hand, is offered to girls from more prosperous families, and with a better education. Usually it specifies that all of the family's main possessions will serve as a pledge until the girl has managed to clear her travel debt with the proceeds of her work. Alternatively, the family may decide to sell some land or its house in order to cover at least part of the money required for the trip.

The madam who first recruits the girl, often in close coopera- tion with her family, entrusts her to another person (usually a trafficker trusted by the 'sponsor') to take her to Europe. From that moment, the madam acts as guarantor for the girl's loyalty to the sponsor, to whom she periodically sends some of the money she manages to earn abroad. A large percentage of this is handed over to the 'sponsor', until the whole debt is repaid, and a much lower percentage goes to the girl's parents. Although the girl's relationship with her family remains very close, supported by the sending of letters and packages as well as telephone calls, it is the Nigerian madam who, for better or worse, acts as the main intermediary with the family. For better when everything is going to plan: the girl is working, and so the family is entitled to a small percentage of her earnings. For worse when the girl is not behaving as expected: the family is then on the receiving end of threats and retaliation. In Nigeria, madams are often in a position to subject the family to heavy pressure and blackmail.

Let us continue with the girls. Once the agreement has been reached, the luckier ones receive the necessary exit papers (real or forged), a visa, a ticket to Europe, and at least £1,000 to declare at passport control. The girl is informed in advance of the precise journey; if the passport is false, she is told how to sign as the person in whose name it is made out; and sometimes she is also taught to memorize the telephone numbers of people to contact in Europe.

At first, as we have seen, the migratory flow from Nigeria followed formally legal routes, but now the women are nearly always in possession of temporary visas and forged identity papers, such as the passport of a citizen of a neighbouring African country. Corrupt practices are widespread in the European embassies of Nigeria and other African countries, especially Ghana, Ivory Coast and South Africa. In Nigeria, many organizations specialize in the production of false documents, each one being used by a trafficker for trips by different girls.

As things stand, women must face long and difficult journeys to reach Europe: for example, one route to Italy and France also passes through Britain. Tighter controls at Lagos airport have further complicated matters, since a scandal a few years ago revealed the corruption of several people working at the Italian embassy. The new routes go at least in part through Africa, where checks at land borders are few and far between. The longest journey crosses the whole of northern Africa, passing through northern Nigeria,

Niger and Mali on the way to the Sahara, then North Africa and on to Spain, France and Italy. A number of shorter land routes take women to the airports of neighbouring countries, and in fact it is quite common for these to be used as a way of avoiding checks for a flight to a European capital (Gramegna 1999). One such 'trail', with a driver-bodyguard always in attendance, takes girls to Mali or Burkina Faso, where they catch a flight bound for Europe. Other routes pass through Abidjan, the capital of Ivory Coast, or Accra, the capital of Ghana, where the women are sometimes entertained and 'shown the ropes' before boarding a plane to Brussels, Paris, Vienna, Madrid, Lisbon or Athens – all of which have been identified as European arrival or transit points. In Britain and the Netherlands, a flow of under-age Nigerian girls has been reported to Italy and France (Terre des Hommes 2001; Wolthius and Blaak 2002). In some cases, the migrants first head for Moscow or another major city in Eastern or Central Europe, before travelling by various routes to Slovenia and across the border into Italy. In other cases, Bosnia features as a major stage in the journey. The Nigerian rings are certainly well organized, then, and it seems that in the large European cities there is always one capable of receiving the girls and arranging a train journey to their final destination. Nigerian organized crime is well known in Europe and elsewhere for its exceptional capacity to link together groups in different countries, through what recent studies have shown to be veritable secret sects, which are much feared in Nigeria, and that can provide cover for illegal trafficking.

While the length of the journey to Europe is at the root of the women's social and cultural deracination, their travel debt (the contracting of which marks the point of no return) is an indispensable corollary. Turning the difficulties to account, the 'sponsors', traffickers and madams all charge exorbitant prices to organize the journey and the woman's reception in the destination country; the debt then ties her life to those of the 'sponsor' and his accomplices – for so long as it remains unpaid. It has been calculated that the organization of one woman's trip may cost between $4,000 and $5,000, while the debt she has to repay to the madam (the only amount that counts for her) varies between $20,000 and $30,000, but can rise as high as $45,000.[13] Clearly the debt does not correspond to the travel expenses: usurious rates of interest are therefore being applied to the initial figure. The girls become aware of the real size of the debt only when they reach their destination, and by then it is too late to turn back. One girl summed this up very well: 'I was a long way from home, penniless and without papers, and with a huge debt. I wanted to call home and ask my family for help, but what help could they give?' (Kennedy and Nicotri 1999: 22). The debt is immediately used as a pretext to confiscate the girl's papers and to insert her into the round of exploitation already prepared for her. Her only solution is to knuckle under and try to earn enough to shake off the debt.

Exploitation in Italy

Thanks to the work of investigators and magistrates, we now know how the system of exploitation works in Italy. The female inductors essentially play a middle role between the girls and the madams in Nigeria – or, if there is none, between the girls and the 'sponsor' who funded their emigration.[14] The main job of the local madam is to maximize the yield from each girl so as to send the debt repayment to her Nigerian counterpart, while also pocketing something extra for herself. To this end, she runs not only the prostitution activity but also the daily lives of the women in her charge. Sometimes, if she is clever enough, she will manage to serve as a go-between with other madams operating on Italian soil, so that her role then becomes one of receiving the girls and immediately selling them to another madam. In Rome in February 2000, a case came to light in which a madam had received at least two hundred women from Nigeria in the space of a few years, and sold each one on for roughly €25,000.

A madam who personally controls girls for prostitution – no more than four to five at a time – has various ways of making them compliant: when they arrive, she takes their passport, money and all personal effects, including the telephone numbers of people they might contact in Europe. Subsequently, to ensure the maximum obedience of the 'children' (as they are known in slang), the madam may employ not only threats but also magic rituals. She is always held in great awe, since the girls depend on her for their daily existence, and besides she takes and manages all the money they earn. If she thinks it appropriate, she can hand a girl over to another madam at any moment, even to one in another country. In some court records, the madams appear as veritable business managers, using their contacts abroad and constantly travelling between towns and regions to check up on 'joints' and street rackets to which the girls can be switched. The madams who amass the biggest fortunes may run several different markets at once, with the help of one or more trustworthy accomplices or 'controllers' to whom they can delegate some of their responsibilities. These controllers are usually women who, having paid off their own debt and demonstrated their abilities, manage to upgrade their position within the organization. They deal with such matters as the upkeep of apartments, food expenditure, the allocation of girls to various places, the collection of money from 'outsiders' using the prostitution 'joints', the vetting of new intakes, the handing out (and careful counting) of condoms.[15]

As in the case of Albanian gangs, African women subject to a similar system must pay over the odds for anything they need, whether they work in the streets or indoors: such things as the hire of a bed, the right to occupy a street corner, the 'joint' rental, the condoms, the special devices and clothing. The 'joint' usually costs the girl between €250 and €300 a month, and she has to pay more or less the same again for a bed in a crowded apartment. All the regular and exceptional costs of subsistence, including such extras as medical or legal fees, have to be paid by the girls themselves, with money deducted from their earnings or added to their debt. There is also a clearly defined system of fines for the slightest offence or shortcoming – for example, if a girl earns too little, or wears unsuitable clothes, or shows up somewhere late. These too are added to the debt, and ensure that it is paid off as slowly as possible. In fact, the time needed to repay the debt varies with both the original amount and the girl's earnings: it can be anywhere between a few months and three or four years or more. As one girl observed, the speed at which she earns money depends not so much on the number of customers as on the type of services she performs: the riskier these are (for example, unprotected sex or sado-masochistic practices), the more she is paid.

The only purpose of the 'children's' duties, then, is to pay back their debt. When one of them finally clears it, she has to organize a party at which she is also expected to give the madam a present, usually a piece of jewellery worth around €1,000. This sets the social seal on the young woman's recovery of freedom, when there should no longer be any obstacles to her setting up as an independent prostitute and saving enough to return to Nigeria; she may then encourage other girls to follow her example and even become a procuress. As we have seen, however, some of the women who regain their freedom begin to run other groups of girls on behalf of the madam, and some may even recruit girls on their own account. For this reason, it has become more and more common in Italy for the madam to report women without a residence permit as soon as they have cleared their debt; their deportation then removes a potential rival and creates space for other girls to be brought in.[16]

The madams operating in Italy generally seem to find it easy to reach an understanding with one another, and this quality enables them to solve many important issues relating to the division of prostitution 'joints' and other business matters. The defensive aspect of their alliance clearly emerges in the face of a challenge from the justice system. Recently, for example, when criminal proceedings were started after the murder of a 'child', the police monitored a meeting among madams convened to work out how to stop girls from testifying in court against one of their 'colleagues'.

Evidence from telephone tapping also shows that one of the madams' main activities is to develop contacts in Italy and Nigeria that will provide the necessary travel documents and residence permits. The papers are usually sent by mail from Nigeria, while in Italy people can be paid to make false statements that facilitate the issuing of a residence permit and the renting of a flat as accommodation or for the purposes of prostitution.

Other economic activity induced by trafficking

The commercial circuits

The above examples illustrate the existence of rings that keep pouring women onto the market, as part of a consolidated system of commercial distribution and clearly defined exploitation. Over time, criminal organizations from different ethnic and geographical backgrounds have managed to occupy particular niches in the global and European markets: in the case of Europe, Albanian and Nigerian groups among those which dominate the supply and exploitation of cheaper sectors, while Russians tend to concentrate on upmarket brothels, Thais hold their corner in the sauna and massage parlour business, sometimes replacing fellow Thais with women from other ethnic groups, and Moldovan rings specialize in supplying women to Middle Eastern markets. In the United States, Russian, Lithuanian and other ex-Soviet groups have managed to capture a large slice of the market, while other parts are controlled by Thais, Chinese and Mexicans. But, although trafficking still presents a diversified picture, and although the trends are highly dynamic, the ever clearer degrees of specialization are undoubtedly a sign of stabilization and greater 'maturity' of the market as a whole.

We have seen that a number of different activities must be coordinated to complete a full cycle from recruitment to final exploitation. Women must first be located and recruited in the countries of origin, or bought when they are already en route. Then it is necessary to organize their transfer to the centres of the commercial sex market, using the services of people able to obtain real or forged documents, or of smugglers or ferrymen who can organize the illegal crossing of frontiers. In the countries of transit, or the destination countries, the women must be persuaded to work as prostitutes at the cheaper end of the market and to accept being treated as simple commodities. Different techniques are used for this purpose, but they all provide for the application, or threat, of physical or psychological violence, even in cases where the girl knew from the beginning that she was intended for work in the sex market. In fact, the induction techniques of trafficking are such that the girls' entry into these prostitution rings is always forced. The crucial stage in this process is always marked by a 'rite of passage': in Nigeria, this may be a much-feared religious ritual, while in Eastern Europe it may involve collective rape and sale at an auction. Once the girl – by force of circumstance, by survival instinct – has submitted to the rules imposed on her, she is put to work by the same traffickers, or else handed over to people in charge of the various circuits, such as the owners of illegal brothels or video bars, street protection racketeers, managers of massage parlours, or organizers of hotel vice rings.

In the destination country, the launching of new prostitutes does not always take place within rings closely connected to the traffickers: there may be several different forms of exploitation, in different settings, which may often be run by people born in the country. It is not unusual for someone to settle the debt with the trafficker in order to obtain full rights over a woman, thereby bringing into being a slavery-like relationship that allows him to have her at his beck and call and to lend her from time to time to male friends. Many women in the Balkans say that they have been victims of this kind of exploitation.

Often, a native-born exploiter buys a girl to put her to work as a prostitute on the streets or in an apartment; owners or managers of illegal places of prostitution may also be interested in this kind of market transaction. An ongoing agreement between such people and foreign clans may indeed be highly profitable. As Operation Pabail revealed, human trafficking to London from Lithuania, Moldova and other Eastern European countries was managed by a woman who obtained travel documents and false identity papers. When the women arrived, they were taken and 'educated' in Acton, West London, before being forced into prostitution. They were controlled by means of fear and coercion, with threats to their families and a system of fines for any breach of the rules. Their travel debt was multiplied by the costs of board and lodging, and the women were exploited in five brothels (Home Office 2004: 78).

The ancillaries

The groups running prostitution rackets generally establish close contacts within the society in which they operate, and cooperation has developed everywhere between foreign and indigenous organizations. There is always a variety of human types who remain in the shadows, only occasionally brought to light by thorough judicial investigations. We know from these, for example, that the complicity of local people – who may not belong to the criminal underworld – is also necessary for the more simply structured kinds of sex exploitation ring.

To be assured of some business continuity, and therefore to be able to invest, foreign exploiters first of all need to regularize their own residence status. There are two possibilities: either an expensive 'fake' marriage with a citizen of the host country, or, more commonly, the purchase of false employment credentials from the owner of a commercial firm or business. Another practical requirement is to have a certain number of mobile phones, and for this purpose there are people willing to buy GSM cards in their own name for a fee of €250. The racketeers must also be in a position to put up 'their' girls in hotels and apartments, and for this they persuade hotel owners to register the presence of only one girl in three, or pay an extra commission for 'reliable' estate agents to turn a blind eye and make false statements to the owner of an apartment.

In Italy there are cases where a Nigerian ring, entirely run by women, uses men of various nationalities to drive the girls by car from place to place. But it is always African men, mostly Nigerians, who serve as bodyguards and carry out acts of intimidation as the need arises. Similarly, it is always co-nationals who are given the job of exporting goods and capital. For, unless 'money transfer' services are used, any capital for repatriation is usually invested in the form of powerful cars to be taken to Nigeria.

In the transit countries, forms of participation in the 'trafficking economy' grow *pari passu* with the trafficking rings themselves. For Nigerian women, the journey involves a number of fixed points of support to which they must refer before they reach their final destination. As we have seen, the en route lodging and control system in the Balkans is highly organized, and a lot of people may intervene in various capacities to help the Slav girls on their way. In fact, it is not difficult to find someone who, for a fee, will make his own minivan available or occasionally serve as a driver or bodyguard. Nor is it difficult to rent for a few days someone's abandoned country cottage, or even city apartment, or to find a hotel owner prepared (for a sum) to allow his premises to be filled with girls on sale to the highest bidder. The long journeys that carry women from remote provinces to the top sex markets offer a large circle of people, including frontier officials and corrupt policemen, considerable and often unexpected opportunities to make a tidy sum on the side. In the *Trafficking in Persons Annual Report* issued by the US State Department, the corruption of officials in Albania, Serbia, Ukraine and many other countries is considered one of the main causes of the spread of trafficking (US Department of State 2004). But little emphasis is placed on embassy corruption in the destination countries, which confidential sources claim to be one of the basic resources for high-grade traffickers.

Money transfers to the countries of origin

The interests connected with sex trafficking and the exploitation of prostitution are equally broad in the countries of origin. As far as Nigeria is concerned, we have already spoken of the outwardly clean and respectable 'sponsors' who put up the initial funds, but whose money-laundering activity is not so well known. According to international experts, the large-scale traffickers generally prefer to reinvest and recycle capital in the richest economies, channelling it through a variety of banking networks and offshore financial centres. To be more precise, investigations have shown that capital accumulated by Nigerians moves within a circuit of professional couriers and 'money transfer' services, whose beneficiaries do not necessarily live in Nigeria, or even Africa, but may reside anywhere in Europe (especially Italy and the Netherlands) or the United States and Canada. It often happens that the proceeds are reinvested in drugs trafficking or other highly lucrative illegal activity, usually not in the impoverished region where the women originated. Indeed, experts note that the trafficking economy rarely brings prosperity or economic benefits to the communities of origin.

At local level, however, numerous interests are active in connection with the women's departure and residence in a rich country, from which they often send back considerable sums of money. Whereas little information is available about Albania or Russia, we know from Nigerian sources that an amazing range of activities and a considerable movement of resources have developed around this migratory flow (Ofuoku 1999). First of all there is the official movement of money: it seems that the constant traffic of parcels to and from Europe creates feverish activity at the central post office in Benin City; and the Western Union office that handles money transfers from Europe is reputed to be the busiest in the whole of Nigeria. Propitiatory activity (much of it in return for payment) is quite intense before and after a woman's departure, as priests offer prayers, oracles predict her future abroad, and traditional doctors use voodoo to bind her to her promises. But, above all else, the Nigerian press focuses on cash remittances from young women abroad, which are changing the look of whole districts of Benin City. Many of the old houses have been demolished and replaced with brand-new buildings. As one representative of the local religious authority put it: 'These people have helped the city to grow. The cars and buses you see were bought with their labour, whether it was legitimate or involved prostitution' (Ofuoku 1999). It appears that in Benin City 'Italo' girls – those few who have successfully returned from Italy – now form part of the top elite. The broad social recognition they enjoy is clear from the success of the film *Glamour Girls 2*, which paints a sensationalist and captivating picture of commercial sex in Europe. The brothers and sisters of these 'Italos' go to the best schools, and at funerals and other ceremonies their families stand out by the splendour of their dress. It is likely, however, that this status attaches to women who have been active not merely in prostitution but in the organization of a vice ring, and who continue to play an entrepreneurial role in one. The return of such women with visible wealth has a stimulating effect on the whole business, as it encourages other families to push their girls to leave.

It is largely due to this living proof of success that second and subsequent waves of departures occur. The dynamic is common throughout the world, wherever recruiters linked to criminal organizations comb and depopulate whole areas looking for young women, as in Nigeria or Russia. Isoken, a Nigerian woman, puts it as follows:

> I got married, but now I am separated. I have two children, who now live with my parents. I decided to come [to Europe] because not a single girl was left in my neighbourhood; they had all gone to Europe and were sending money back to help their parents.
> (Kennedy, Nicotri 1999: 122–3)

In the former Soviet Union, especially in regions where infant mortality has been low or falling, serious demographic imbalances have appeared which will certainly have repercussions for future generations. Moldova, one of these regions, is pervaded with the myth of girls who have made a fortune. Those who return become a model to emulate, partly because they tend to give a positive image of themselves and try to recruit others. The recruiter who has already worked abroad, and who is therefore more capable of persuading other girls, is a well-known figure even in Thailand and is becoming more and more familiar in the Balkans. It is already widespread throughout Eastern Europe, and in Ukraine it is estimated that 70 per cent of new recruitment is done by women.

Systematic studies of the girls' return to their homeland are generally still lacking.[17] According to people working in the field of assistance, the ways in which they are perceived, and welcomed, vary quite widely; the basic rules seem to be the same as for migrants everywhere, though with some much more pronounced features. Someone who comes back a 'winner' is treated very differently from someone who comes back a 'loser'. People returning to their homeland are usually accepted and recognized by their original community only if they have sent money home during their period abroad, or if they have visibly struck it rich; the community does not then look too closely at the sources of the wealth, or at least does not ask too many questions. In any event, those who return without a guaranteed income are at a clear disadvantage. Usually, they do not live in their area of origin but prefer to settle in a city, as they find it impossible to recognize themselves in their previous identity or lifestyle. A woman returning home unlucky, who is poor and perhaps sick, is made to feel ashamed and may even be rejected by her own family,[18] while the social disrepute exposes her to frequent sexual harassment by men.

Notes

1. According to CIA estimates. Cf. O'Neill-Richard 2000.
2. Data concerning these flows are based on IOM research, some of which has been published in the bulletin *Trafficking in Migrants*. For

an overview of the main areas of trafficking in women from East-Central Europe, see Monzini 2004.

3. See IOM, *Trafficking in Migrants*, Autumn 2000: 22.

4. See the data presented by Arta Mandro, Albanian deputy justice minister, to the IOM workshop on trafficking: 30 November 1999, Farnesina Palace, Rome.

5. This information, taken from court records (Tribunale di Milano 1999a), is confirmed by magistrates and experts in the field. Currently, according to police sources, the price at which women are sold on the Roma market is also between €1,500 and €2,000.

6. See Procura Distrettuale Antimafia, L'Aquila 1999.

7. This picture clearly emerges from statements made in Italy and recorded by agencies investigating human trafficking.

8. It has been known for girls to arrive in Italy after passing through the hands of as many as fifteen 'owners'.

9. Indeed, Nigeria occupies third position in the world for the number of its citizens arrested abroad.

10. If the business took hold fastest in Italy, this was probably because the African component represented a novelty there, whereas it had already been present in the markets of northern Europe, and in multiethnic countries such as France.

11. We do not know how much this interest amounts to. Although the Italian police and magistracy have now completed a major study of the Italian side of the business, poor cooperation between the two countries on justice issues means that no international investigations have been carried out.

12. See the website of the Women's Consortium of Nigeria.

13. The prices vary considerably. Some madams buy girls in Italy for $6,000, and some debts can be around $20,000: see Questura di Udine 2000.

14. Sometimes the husband of a madam active in Italy may help to recruit girls back in Nigeria.

15. The counting of condoms is a way of checking how many men a girl has been with. It is hard for them to cheat about this, because they know the high price they would have to pay if the slightest fraud was uncovered.

16. As we have seen, the same practices are used with Thai and Filipino women (David and Monzini 1999).

17. Studies do exist, however, of regions where the phenomenon has

been known for a long time. For the Dominican Republic, see
Sleightholme and Sinha 1996, and IOM 1996b, which stresses the
socially marginal positions occupied by women who have worked
abroad as prostitutes. For Thailand, see Phongpaichit 1982.

18. Another effect of trafficking, already visible in Ukraine, may be
the prevalence of AIDS. In Russia and Central Asia, too, although
other causes are also in play, HIV infections are spreading rapidly
in the population. Experts consider that this precipitous rise will
continue, given the inadequacy of public information and prevention
campaigns.

4

Prevention and opposition:
instruments and policies

Ways of controlling prostitution

The debate on prostitution is thick with moral tension and goes
hand in hand with reflection about the ethical basis of prostitution
itself. In this respect, the Convention for the Suppression of the
Traffic in Persons and of the Exploitation of the Prostitution of
Others, passed by the UN General Assembly in 1949, set out an
important goal. Under the terms of this convention, neither those
who prostitute themselves nor their customers shall be punishable:
the crime liable to prosecution is 'exploitation of the prostitution
of others'. The underlying philosophy, then, accepts prostitution only if it is the result of a personal, private choice. Being
incompatible with the dignity and value of the human person,
prostitution is not considered an economic activity on a par with
all others. Therefore it must not 'invade' the social space: its external manifestations, such as soliciting, may be harmful to public
morality and should be punished. Within this general theoretical
framework, the 1949 Convention called on governments to develop
ways of intervening in society, through campaigns of prevention

and assistance for women intending to give up prostitution, and to enact suitable legislation for the suppression of all forms of exploitation.

More than fifty years later, the balance sheet is far from satisfactory; things have not worked out as the Convention intended. First of all, it was ratified by only 72 of the 185 member states of the United Nations, and its implementation has not been the object of any monitoring and verification mechanism. It is true that new legislation in the 1950s and 1960s helped to reduce the incidence of exploitation, but in the last twenty years prostitution has been spreading on a scale that would have been unthinkable in the 1940s, and exploitation, including in its most violent forms, has staged a major comeback. Today, there is no concerted international approach to the problem, and legislation shows wide variations around the world. The larger countries that modelled new laws on the Convention – for example, France, Italy and Britain – developed so-called 'abolitionist' systems, which sought, with greater or lesser success, to eliminate state regulation of prostitution. In other countries, such as the USA (except Nevada), some states of Nigeria and Thailand, prostitution was simply outlawed and those who went on regardless are punished. In the case of Sweden it is only the clients who are prosecuted.[1] In other countries the state still regulates prostitution and orders compulsory health checks on people who prostitute themselves, but not on their clients. Some of these systems – the Greek, for example – do not accord any precise rights to those who prostitute themselves, whereas others – such as the German or Dutch – recognize prostitution as a work activity that enjoys the protection of the law.[2]

In all three regimes – which we may define as abolition, prohibition and regulation – the systems of exploitation benefit from illegality and the murky atmosphere in which prostitution takes place. Where such activity is criminal, various forms of exploitation spread with great ease: those who prostitute themselves independently are wide open to blackmail, since they are acting outside the law, and have to find a place within existing systems of protection. Individuals with good underworld links – the exploiters of prostitution – then offer to guarantee a certain continuity in activity; it is thus no accident that in the United States 70 per cent of prostitution is thought to be more or less directly run by organized criminals (Gomez 2001).[3] Forms of exploitation also easily reproduce themselves in countries that choose the 'regulatory' path, including those such as Germany or the Netherlands that offer the greatest personal guarantees. In these two countries, recent laws have further liberalized prostitution by recognizing the legal foundation of the contract between prostitute and customer, and by extending social security entitlements to people who sell sexual services. But these laws apply only to prostitutes with residence in the European Union, so that the great majority of women from outside 'the community' come to form a huge underground market in which price competition is founded on practices often based on forced prostitution.[4] Recently, this trend towards a split between a regular and an underground market has become stronger in the main countries with a system of state regulation: for example, already in 1996 a fall in the number of women working in the 'clean' market was reported in Austria, together with an exponential rise in the illegal market (IOM 1996a). Similarly, in Greece there are thought to be more than 5,000 unregistered prostitutes in Athens alone, against 400 registered (Europap/Tampep 2001), while in Germany estimates put the number of unregistered prostitutes at a minimum of 150,000. Living on the fringes of the law, these women are even less likely than in neighbouring countries to report their exploiters to the authorities. In this model, therefore, one always finds two systems side by side: a 'healthy', controlled one, charging high prices, and a much cheaper illegal one, invisible and totally uncontrolled, where the worst forms of exploitation are practised. The defects are also evident with regard to working conditions. Experiences in Australia and Europe confirm that, although official directives are obeyed in some places, women are forced in others to work without condoms and to comply with everything the clients demand (Home Office 2004: 85).

The abolitionist approach has the great merit of seeing that people who prostitute themselves are prone to various forms of exploitation, and therefore in need of protection. But the kinds of protection that it proposes are actually very weak. Above all, laws with an abolitionist inspiration nearly always reflect a strong social stigma: even when they affirm a right to prostitute oneself on an independent basis, they define it as an activity halfway between legality and illegality, and related forms of behaviour such as soliciting, the aiding and abetting of prostitution or the practice of prostitution in association with others often remain punishable offences. In practice, people who prostitute themselves keep running up against major obstacles that lead them to break one law or another, thereby making themselves vulnerable and open to blackmail. Police apparatuses may in many cases target even the freer forms of prostitution. And, although one of the motives for abolitionist legislation is to protect those who prostitute themselves, the ways in which the law is applied often show that the main objective is to contain prostitution (especially in relation to problems of public order and morality): that is, to defend the state more than to defend individuals who prostitute themselves. With regard to street prostitution, in particular, a number of attempts have been made to create protected zones, or to set aside special areas where the exercise of prostitution is monitored. Here a police presence can increase safety levels, and social or health workers can be on the scene to provide specialist services. Interesting experiments along these lines in Britain (Doncaster and Liverpool), the Netherlands and Italy, partly designed to eliminate public order disturbances (Home Office 2004: 82), deserve to be carefully assessed. For, as European experts have pointed out, any policy that drives prostitution underground makes the women more vulnerable and removes them from the reach of welfare services. On the other side, the various legislative proposals for periodic health checks, official registration and compulsory use of brothels would make the harsh conditions of exploitation even worse, without bringing any benefit to women already working as independent prostitutes. If a decision is made to go for state regulation of the prostitution market, which would mean accepting the commercial value of the activity, then the aim should be to protect the women involved in it, not to bring back an apparatus of police controls and compulsory health checks. Greater scope for prostitutes to organize their own activity on a commercial basis, and greater recognition of it as a possible form of independent work, might help to bring about a change in social perceptions, and a reduction in the social stigma attached to the activity. Perhaps such an approach could point in a constructive direction the changes under way in the social and cultural environment.

At present, the European picture is fairly homogenous in terms of the presence of migrant prostitutes and the associated phenomena of trafficking and exploitation.[5] But it is more diverse in terms of prostitution laws,[6] and partly for that reason there is no debate on the issue in the European Parliament. As a leading expert, MEP Patsy Sorensen, recently said, the debate on human trafficking is the most difficult to pursue within the EU institutions, precisely because it is impossible to find a platform rooted in a common vision. Nevertheless, faced with the spread of ever more brutal forms of organized exploitation, voices from several quarters have stressed the need to strengthen the instruments to fight and prevent such developments. Since 1994, therefore, despite sometimes heated arguments, the EU has officially operated with a distinction between voluntary and forced prostitution, in accordance with the principle of 'freedom of choice'.[7] This lowest common denominator has made it possible to prioritize the struggle against trafficking and forced prostitution. In the United States, on the other hand, the main tendency involves a radical emphasis on what prostitution and trafficking have in common. In December 2002, the National Security Presidential Directive took a strong line against any legalization of prostitution, considering it a dangerous and dehumanizing activity that encourages trafficking and new forms of slavery. Accordingly, the US government refuses to fund the activity of NGOs which, in the spirit of damage limitation, support forms of legalized prostitution abroad.

Destination countries and the struggle against trafficking

In the last few years, there have been a number of important advances in the struggle against trafficking. The United States Congress passed a Trafficking Victims Protection Act in 2000, and an improved Trafficking Victims Protection Reauthorization Act in 2003, which afford various kinds of assistance to the victims of trafficking. In an attempt to reduce its scale, the government has also launched close monitoring operations throughout the world, which result each year in a report listing the activity of each country in this field. Aid sanctions are then imposed on those which display little sensitivity to the issue. The European Union, too, favours legislation that will commit governments to victim protection: the application of the Brussels Declaration, adopted by the Council of Ministers in March 2003, is currently being monitored by an ad hoc group of experts. More generally, a number of working platforms have been adopted throughout the world: in the Balkans and Central Europe, the OSCE and other bodies are coordinating prevention and suppression policies and attempting to boost intergovernmental cooperation; similar regional efforts are going on in some areas of Southeast Asia, Latin America and Africa.[8] In every region, in fact, there is a growing awareness of the centrality of international cooperation on the issue. Considerable progress has also been made in the fight against the sexual exploitation of minors, especially in the sector of the industry linked to tourism. The World Tourism Organization has set up a special task force, and in 1999 it issued a Global Code of Conduct that has led to a growing number of prosecutions of exploiters.

In general, apart from constant appeals to governments to address the problem, the international organizations ask destination countries of the sex trade (most of which have sizeable resources at their disposal) to play a leading role in the global struggle against exploitation and actively to cooperate with the countries of origin and transit to strengthen protective systems, assistance and joint work with local institutions and NGOs. At a theoretical level, there is now a widespread conviction that international cooperation between police forces and judicial apparatuses, and between both of these and agencies or associations working on victim protection, will be necessary to make any local initiative effective. In particular, the United Nations has proposed that various countries of origin, transit and destination should elaborate common policies and legislation capable of having an effect on several fronts. Together with the Convention against Transnational Organized Crime,[9] two additional protocols have addressed the problems of migrant smuggling and human trafficking, especially of women and children. The trafficking protocol, which came into force on 25 December 2003, binds the (currently fifty) states that have signed it to arrange all the necessary instruments for preventive activity, victim protection and an offensive against the criminal core of the business. With regard to the victims – who are defined as such even when they appear to consent to the exploitative relationship – the destination countries are called upon to offer various forms of assistance and integration into society, while the countries of origin are supposed to help with active reintegration of those returning from abroad. Further protection under national penal codes is also envisaged, as is the awarding of compensation out of funds confiscated from traffickers. To strike hard at their interests, the protocols call for special legislation against trafficking and greater bilateral and multilateral cooperation among not only justice systems but also various governmental and civil institutions. The first results of these UN directives have been quite considerable: many countries have passed new legislation against trafficking and for victim protection, even in cases where the victims have contravened immigration laws. However, among the countries which have signed the protocol but not yet ratified it are some of the main destination countries: Germany, Italy, Japan, Thailand, the United Kingdom and the United States.

Nevertheless, it is difficult to tackle the problem of trafficking at an international level, because it is perceived in different ways in the countries of origin, transit and destination. In the destination countries, the need to guarantee the basic human rights of victims often conflicts with other priorities, such as the safeguarding of frontiers against illegal immigration or the prevention of public order offences associated with prostitution. Various governmental bodies and NGOs may have different objectives in view, with the result that police forces and justice systems, social workers and human rights activists often find themselves operating in an uncoordinated manner. For this reason, the principal task for national politicians – and the principal direction of international efforts – is now to harmonize as much as possible the safeguarding of state interests and the protection of victims. As far as the latter is concerned, the main new initiatives have been taken in Europe (first in Italy, Belgium and the Netherlands) and the United States, through changes in immigration law and the introduction of special residence permits for women without valid papers who can show they are subject to serious forms of exploitation. This guarantee, which considerably strengthens the legal position of victims, has already demonstrated its effectiveness, and the model is currently being applied, or discussed as a basis for new legislation, in other parts of the world.

Italy's considerable experience in this field has been recognized as a possible basis for the elaboration of EU victim protection procedures. A strategy against human trafficking was worked out in Italy by a committee of ministerial representatives, NGOs and international organizations, which began by discussing how to define the characteristic features and needs of people subject to trafficking. Once it had been established that their first need was for personal safety, the committee confirmed the right of victims to protection and assistance. The resulting legislation, adopted in July 1998, makes it possible for victims of exploitation to obtain a residence permit and to follow a course of social integration, with the support of structures that are in part publicly funded. Nationwide welfare services, provided by secular and Catholic NGOs, offer a series of stages: assistance in the street by so-called 'mobile units'; accompaniment of girls to regional social service departments; placement in families to strengthen their personal autonomy (especially in the case of minors), or accommodation in residential units or special 'shelters'; and help with integration into the world of work. Public awareness campaigns have also been organized with the aim of prevention, and a telephone helpline provides information and directs callers to special advice centres; it received more than 187,000 calls in the period from July 2000 to March 2001.

Social workers, magistrates and policemen agree that, if it is possible for women to report their exploiters to the authorities, the rings in question try to reduce the risk of defection by treating them in a more tolerable way and giving them a greater economic incentive to stay. It has been found in Europe and the Balkans, for example, that exploiters tend to behave better towards the women once they realize that some payment and an improvement in working conditions reduce the risk of defection. Generally in recent years, the situation has been slowly changing in countries where there is a system of victim support and growing official attention to the problem. Here, the tendency is for traffickers to treat their victims more tolerably, to pay a small wage, and to move the business into private places that look less like prostitution 'joints'. Nevertheless, although intervention by the authorities has partly modified the system, experts report that it still gives serious cause for alarm: extremely harsh situations can still be found, and there is a tendency, in response to police raids, to move the exploitation into apartments, clients' homes and other places where it is no longer visible. After making contact by telephone or on the Internet, customers can visit women in a hotel or apartment in absolute privacy, without any possibility of checks. Some areas of assistance to victims, moreover, remain completely undeveloped. Despite the UN directives to focus action against traffickers and exploiters, the policies aimed at the suppression of trafficking have often made difficult headway. The phenomenon tends to remain hidden, even in countries that have an adequate set of regulations and significant investigative resources. The British authorities, for instance, admit that still too little is known about the real scale of the problem, and the situation cannot improve unless all the relevant bodies, in each country, make it a priority. Besides, efforts to reduce exploitation in some areas may lead to its expansion in others (UK Government 2004). Linda Kelly, who interviewed police officials as part of her research in Britain, reports that only nine police districts are able to quantify the local scale of the phenomenon, and only two of these carry out regular monitoring of the sex markets (Kelly 2002: 12); the inevitable problems therefore remain invisible in many parts of the country, and, as Kelly points out, regular monitoring would anyway be strongly obstructed by those who organize and work in these rings. Many European magistrates believe that investigations are almost never started independently, but only after a victim has reported a case of exploitation to the authorities. Major technical problems may then arise, especially as the contradiction between the great mobility of the sex rings and the territorial limits of those in charge of the investigation means that considerable extra time and effort has to be put into the work of coordination. Language problems, and the frequent lack of suitable interpreters, are compounded by the difficulty of finding reliable opposite numbers to extend an investigation or prosecution in another country. Widespread corruption in the countries of origin or transit is a further obstacle that tends to keep any inquiry limited to the destination country. Should a decision be made to extend it to another country, it is often essential to give adequate protection to the family of the victim who reported her exploiters – yet the appropriate legal instruments may well be lacking for that. Hence, even in countries where victim protection is quite developed, investigative practices pose problems for which it is difficult to find a solution. And, as everywhere else, the difficulty is to take action without causing more harm to the victim.

A further problem is to identify the victims, who are not always evident and often find it very difficult to trust the authorities. The complex relationship with those who control them, their violation of immigration laws, the fact that they came to terms with their own exploiters and are often privy to their involvement in drugs and other illegal business: this all makes them see themselves as deviants, who have no right to be defended. Many women are traumatized by a great sense of guilt, feeling that they are partly to blame for their situation, while others may be tied emotionally to the exploiters themselves. For these reasons, too, it still seems to be the case everywhere in the world that the police too often hit at the women rather than their exploiters. As the OSCE pointed out in a recent report,

> when laws are enforced in destination countries, they are far more likely to be enforced against the trafficked persons than the perpetrators of trafficking crimes. In a typical brothel raid, for example, the police arrest, interrogate, detain and deport the women (for illegal prostitution or for working illegally) while the pimps and brothel owners go virtually unpunished.... Some destination countries, such as the United States and a number of European states, have developed systems to protect victims escaping situations of trafficking. European countries are introducing new laws to combat trafficking flows, and to protect victims. But complete studies are still rare, and the forces of order encounter many difficulties in collecting evidence and arresting the culprits. (OSCE 2001: 19)

Deportation to countries of origin

As things stand today, in the overwhelming majority of destination countries, a woman whose papers are not in order does not have the option to report her exploiter without herself being deported, either at once or (if she formally accuses her exploiter) at the end of the trial. Someone deported in this way for a breach of residence regulations automatically finds herself subject to social rejection in her country of origin. Even in destination countries that have introduced forms of assistance and special residence permits, hundreds of sex workers are deported annually for residence violations. Repatriation treaties with countries of origin make it possible to complete deportation proceedings within forty-eight hours, on the basis of a so-called 'presumption of nationality'.

What happens to the women once they have been repatriated? A small minority receive assistance and help with reintegration, under programmes run by the IOM and other agencies in co-ordination with local NGOs, but the great majority are left to fend for themselves. Given the social stigma attached to prostitution in many countries of origin, the women who return are vulnerable to harsh forms of social exclusion.

In general, the absence of monitoring provisions means that it is difficult to know exactly what happens. According to a Thai study based on personal interviews, even women who had had a certain success abroad, making some money for themselves after repayment of the initial debt, often displayed serious symptoms of a split personality. Though considered brave and successful at home, and in their community of origin, they actually felt fragile, abused and misunderstood. No one could understand the suffering they had endured to earn the little that now belonged to them all, and they found the situation especially painful if these savings were badly invested (Caouette and Saito 1999).

It is more often the case, in the countries of origin, that a strong social stigma attaches to the kind of life that the women have had to lead; their greatest fear, then, is that the truth about their time abroad will become public knowledge. Moreover, if they have not managed to pay off the whole debt, the blackmail and other problems persist. Their return is often traumatic from the start, since they may have boarded the plane or boat with the same clothes that they used to wear on the streets or in a brothel. In Nigeria, no adequate reception facilities exist for the 3–4,000 victims of trafficking who are forcibly repatriated each year.[10] The women are detained for a couple of days while they undergo personal data checks and medical tests – then, if they show no sign of a sexually transmitted disease, they are released and left to their own devices. Usually they do not return to their village of origin, and without money they do not even have the means to go from Lagos to their home country in Edo state. Often they remain in the capital, where they end up prostituting themselves to earn some money to send to their children or parents, or to pay off the last of their debt. Often they again fall prey to a vice ring. In any event, unless the time abroad has had the hoped-for impact on their long-term prospects, they may easily face the (painful) choice of leaving again, or of recruiting other women, perhaps even relatives, to keep the money coming in. Similar mechanisms are at work in other countries of origin. It should also be borne in mind that the speed of deportation tends to be matched by similar speed in the response of the traffickers. In Moldova, once a girl on her way back has been through passport control at the airport, a friend of her exploiter may already be waiting to take control of her again. Such cases are very common, and as many as 25 per cent of girls assisted by the IOM find themselves being trafficked a second time (IOM 2004a). In general, it is very dangerous to help girls who have been repatriated, because they are still considered their owner's property and will return to exploitation rings with the same group of traffickers. Once back in their country of origin, they may also have to face the additional problem of repaying the homeward travel costs to their exploiters.

Problems in the countries of origin have begun to receive greater official attention since the first international programmes came into operation. With regard to victim support, some projects are in place to fund the voluntary return of women, while others, usually run by international NGOs and funded by donor countries or the European Union, are creating rehabilitation and reintegration structures in the countries of origin. In Albania, for example, international organizations and NGOs have been working together to open special shelters for girls who cannot return to their home country in Eastern Europe, and for Albanian girls repatriated from elsewhere in Europe. Other initiatives are currently under way in Moldova, Ukraine, Romania and the Balkans, whereas in Russia the situation is marked by a serious shortage of appropriate centres (none at all in Moscow for women in this situation). Moreover, despite the efforts, assistance programmes have only a weak impact on the overall situation, since repatriation to East European and Balkan countries of origin continues at a rapid rate.

The most positive signs in the countries of origin concern the inevitable priority of victim protection, rather than the prevention or suppression of trafficking. With regard to protection, it is now urgently necessary to move to a higher level of strategic, 'systemic' action, which addresses the social-economic conditions and gender discrimination that drive young women from certain regions to leave without adequate safeguards. A carefully planned shift of resources to local level, through such mechanisms as decentralized cooperation, among others, might lead to considerable improvements in certain regions with a high rate of departure. Apart from micro-credit projects and other initiatives to improve the daily lives of women, there is also a need for training courses and information campaigns geared to would-be emigrants.

On the suppression of trafficking, several organizations have stressed the need to strengthen judicial cooperation and to conduct transnational investigations. This is a difficult but not impossible task, even if, in the view of local observers, the main problem today in Nigeria or Albania, Moldova or Ukraine, is the high degree of protection enjoyed by traffickers. In the case of Albania, anyone from a minister or civil servant to the head of a family may turn out to have an economic stake in the business; it involves many different people and mobilizes capital from important investors, and the corruption reaches right to the top of the ruling hierarchies.[11] The same is true in all the main countries of origin, where criminal prosecution is much more common against prostitutes than traffickers. It is true that some countries have begun to give greater emphasis to the question and to introduce important reforms: in Ukraine, for example, an interministerial panel has been set up along Italian lines, while in Poland a new law has made human trafficking a criminal offence, and in the Czech Republic the national police now have a special investigation department capable of taking part in international operations. Even in these countries, however, repatriation or deportation is the most widely practised solution, and NGOs report that women from Eastern Europe to whom it is applied also encounter serious difficulties (Horbunova 1999). Often they no longer have a passport, and their embassy, instead of paying for a ticket back home, usually asks train or coach operators to give the women free passage. The women therefore have no guarantee that they will be able to complete the trip without problems, either en route or at the various border controls. Nor are they given a right to privacy, since journalists, as has happened in Nigeria, can bombard them with intrusive questions. Trafficking victims who return to the Balkans by ship from Turkey, via Odessa or Russia, suffer harassment and physical or verbal violence from frontier guards, who may demand sexual services from women without proper papers (as do ticket collectors from those unable to buy a ticket) (IOM 2004a: 95). In general, once the women have arrived back, they choose not to denounce their exploiters or to cooperate with the local police. Unless special protection is available, they prefer to change their name and address and to simplify their life by drawing a line under what has happened to them.

Notes

1. A law passed in Sweden in 1999 punishes clients with up to six months' imprisonment, which may be commuted to a course of therapy with the social services department. Prostitution is thus seen as a social problem that should be reduced as much as possible, a form of violence reflecting the obsolete gender roles of a patriarchal order.

2. A clear picture of the legislation in each country may be gained from the website of 'The Protection Project', at the John F. Kennedy School of Government, Washington DC, which presents a database on national and international systems for the protection of women and children from commercial sexual exploitation, including forms of trafficking and forced prostitution.

3. A good example may be found in Ken Russell's film *Whore*, which graphically depicts the operation of these mechanisms.

4. In Germany, where it is estimated that at least 50 per cent of prostitutes are foreign, the associations that defend prostitutes' rights have demanded an immediate end to repressive measures against foreigners, such as police roundups, compulsory HIV tests, police questioning without an interpreter, and summary deportation of women without a work permit.

5. For a survey of European countries, see Lehti 2003.

6. Not only ambiguities but also profound national differences in the legislative regulation of prostitution play a major role in the weakness of migrants entering the market, for the women in question often have confused ideas about what the law actually says in their destination country. This is especially true of women who travel around a lot or are kept in semi-confinement, without any clear awareness of their rights.

7. According to the definition, forced prostitution includes any situation where women are forced to prostitute themselves following acts of physical or moral violence, or are deceived about the nature of the work they are expected to perform.

8. For detailed information on the various regions, see the proceedings of the meeting on 'Improving Data and Research on Human Trafficking', organized by the IOM, 27–28 March 2004, Rome.

9. The Convention was submitted in December 2000, in Palermo, for member states to sign. The text may be found at www.odccp.

org/crime_cicp.

10. See 'Africa: Government Signs Pact with UN on Human Trafficking', *Vanguard*, 4 May 2002.

11. On this whole issue, see 'Welcome, Dear Prostitutes', an article by a group of eight Albanian journalists, which appeared on 7 February 2002 in the weekly *Klan*.

Concluding remarks

Human trafficking and the exploitation of prostitution is a business founded on violence and blackmail, but at the same time it plays on the hopes and expectations of those involved in it. There are the expectations of the girls and young women who emigrate from socially and economically deprived regions of the world. Sometimes they are deceived about the kind of work in store for them, but sometimes they knowingly agree to work in the entertainment or prostitution industry, because they think that in the long term this will allow them to improve the living conditions of themselves and their family. There are the expectations of the traffickers and 'middlemen', who recruit girls and young women, arrange their trip and organize their exploitation in the richest sex markets of the world, acting with great ruthlessness to derive the maximum profit from them. And there are the expectations of the customers, who are on the lookout for sometimes 'extraordinary' sexual services at a moderate cost. Quite a large part of the commercial sex market has recently remodelled itself as an international business under the pressure of these different forces. In fact, as we have seen, the business only fulfils some of the initial expectations: it brings great benefits to all except the girls and women.

According to the feminist author Kathleen Barry, it is not prostitution but the exploitation of prostitution that is the world's oldest profession. We can agree that she is more or less right. Of course, its connotations have differed considerably: in our own society, which is becoming ever more multiethnic, exploitation sometimes takes the extreme form of trafficking, whose victims are in their great majority foreign women. As we have seen, young female migrants may be attracted, deluded, tricked or snared into the cheapest sectors of prostitution, at any point in their trip: still inside the country of origin or in a transit or destination country. Structures have now taken shape that may be said to constitute a veritable 'woman market'. The growing interest of organized crime in human trafficking and the exploitation of prostitution demonstrates that there is fertile terrain for it at the heart of our global civilization. It has become an economic system perfectly integrated into the wider circuit of prostitution.

Nevertheless, in all the international organizations, the discussion of trafficking tries to skate round the difficult issue of prostitution. This may involve a diplomatic choice, to avoid clashing with any of three main strategies (abolition, regulation, prohibition). But one practical consequence of this reticent behaviour – which probably also has to do with the fact that most policymakers are male – is that few studies on the issue of prostitution have been funded in recent years, and only a few investigations have been stimulated into particular cases at a national or comparative level. Although some interest in the demand side is beginning to emerge within EU projects, for example, the lack of detailed analysis and clear information has until now hindered the development of long-term action programmes to combat the worst forms of exploitation.

These forms of exploitation could be better fought within their relevant framework – that is, the framework of prostitution. Yet the economic aspects of 'trafficking' have not yet been studied in a structured manner: various research projects have centred on the victims of trafficking, but no specific analysis has focused on the organization of the market and the demand side sustaining it. The centre of attention today is the trafficking and movement of women. At an international level, the greatest energies are devoted to the issues of transport and enslavement, while much less is done to understand how exploitation functions in the destination countries. Operations to combat trafficking follow the same logic. The very adoption of the term 'trafficking in human beings for sexual exploitation' – which, as we have seen, includes every stage of the process, from initial recruitment to final exploitation – indicates that no specific attention has been given to exploitation mechanisms in the countries of arrival. Yet these are the crucial mechanisms that have to be understood, because they are the ones underpinning the accumulation of capital. In other words, the emphasis in today's debates is placed on trafficking and traffickers, and not enough on the actual ways in which women are exploited. For example, although the range of places where prostitution is practised (e.g. video bars and clubs) has evidently increased in recent years, little or nothing has been written on the forms of exploitation that occur there. The studies that do examine these settings usually do so within one of two contrasting perspectives. Some seek to show that prostitution can be a valid choice, that only a minority of women who prostitute themselves in a foreign country are victims of trafficking, and that, despite many contradictions and great suffering, many do succeed in working out a plan in keeping with their own ambitions in life (Thorbek and Pattanaik 2002). Other studies, such as that of O'Connell Davidson, argue the opposite: they reveal the forms of exploitation undergone by women who seem to enjoy cast-iron guarantees. More generally, the debates on trafficking and prostitution take place on different levels. When the two issues are not rolled into one – which is still very often the case – the links between them are unlikely to be satisfactorily analysed.

It is not possible to develop the best solutions to trafficking by basing oneself on the best practices of the past, partly because there is still no study of what caused the 'white slave trade' to wither away in the first half of the twentieth century. We know that this was a slow process: the problem was still present at the end of the Second World War, in 1949, when the United Nations drafted its Convention for the Suppression of the Traffic in Persons and of the Exploitation of the Prostitution of Others. Of course, the gradual decline in the exploitation of prostitution was subsequently encouraged not only by reforms in the regulation of prostitution in the colonies but also by social-economic changes resulting from decolonization. In many countries of the world, women had greater opportunities to influence political choices, or at least greater scope to 'have their say'. Today, grassroots social movements and NGOs have acquired greater strength and play a much more important role than before in actively promoting reforms. The circles in civil society that fight the exploitation of prostitution are still mostly organized by women, but a further impetus could come from men's energies that are still too little in evidence. Indeed, a comparison of the diverse (and mostly unexpressed) positions emerging in the male world would give a crucial spur to our understanding of the phenomenon. Only in the context of such a debate would it be possible to grasp the extent to which certain political solutions on offer actually reflect the interests of certain customers – interests that usually conceal themselves behind a façade of spurious moralism or public order issues.

Bibliography

Ahmad, N. (2001) *In Search of Dreams: Study on the Situation of the Trafficked Women & Children from Bangladesh and Nepal to India*, Dhaka: International Organization for Migration.

Anarfi, J.K. (1998) 'Ghanaian Women and Prostitution in Côte d'Ivoire', in K.J. Kempadoo and J. Doezema (eds), *Global Sex Workers: Rights, Resistance and Redefinition*, London: Routledge.

Anderson, B., and O'Connell Davidson, J. (2003) *Is Trafficking in Human Beings Demand Driven? A Multi-Country Pilot Study*, Migration Research Series No. 15, Geneva: International Organization for Migration.

Annan, K. (2002) 'Il mondo diviso dalla povertà', *La Repubblica*, 4 February.

Arieff, I. (2000) 'U.N. Insists No Police Ties to Bosnia Prostitution', Reuters, 5 March.

Aronowitz, A.A. (2001) 'Smuggling and Trafficking in Human Beings: The Phenomenon, the Markets that Drive it and the Organizations that Promote it', *European Journal on Criminal Policy and Research*, vol. 9, no. 2, Summer.

Aslanov, E. (2002) 'Krasnodar Sex Trade Booming', *Reporting Online*, Institute for War & Peace, 5 April.

Associazione Parsec (ed.) (1998) *Il traffico di donne immigrate per sfruttamento sessuale: aspetti e problemi. Ricerca e analisi della situazione italiana, spagnola e greca e interventi sociali nel settore, rapporto di ricerca*, Rome: Programma Dafne, University of Florence.

Baden, S. (1999) 'Gender, Governance and the Feminization of Poverty', Background Paper No. 2, 'Women and Political Participation: 21st Century Challenges', meeting organized by the United Nations Development Program, New Delhi, 24–26 March.

Bales, K. (1999a) *Disposable People: New Slavery in the Global Economy*, Berkeley: University of California Press.

Bales, K. (1999b) 'Globalization and Slavery', *International Dialogue* 1, Summer.

Barlay, S. (1975) *Sex Slavery*, rev. edn, London: Coronet Books.

Barry, K. (1979) *Female Sexual Slavery*, New York: New York University Press.

Barry, K. (1995) *Prostitution of Sexuality*, New York: New York University Press.

Bassey, O. (2000) 'Human Trafficking: 454 Nigerians Deported', *This Day, Africa News Online*, 3 August.

Bertone, A.M. (2000) 'Sexual Trafficking in Women: International Political Economy and the Politics of Sex', *Gender Issues*, Winter.

Bibes, P. (2001) *The Status of Human Trafficking in Latin America*, Washington DC: Transnational Crime and Corruption Center.

Bindel, J., and Kelly, L. (2004) *A Critical Examination of Responses to Prostitution in Four Countries: Victoria–Australia, Ireland, the Netherlands and Sweden*, Glasgow: Routes Out.

Bouamama, S. (2004) 'L'homme en question, le processus du devenir client de la prostitution', paper for Mouvement du Nid, Paris, October.

Bradanini, A. (1999) Paper presented at the International Conference on Trafficking in Human Beings and the Role of Organized Crime, organized by UNODC and UNICRI, Naples, 27–29 May.

Brussa, L. (1999) 'Introduzione: le politiche europee', in Associazione on the Road (ed.), *Terre di mezzo. Esperienze ipotesi utopie nel Pianeta Prostituzione, Atti e sviluppi di un convegno*, Capodarco di Fermo.

Butterwek, B. (1999) 'Trafficking of Women and Girls for Prostitution: The Case of Central Europe', paper presented at the international conference 'New Frontiers of Crime: Trafficking in Human Beings and New Forms of Slavery', organized by UNICRI, Verona, 22–23 October.

Cabral, G.V. (2001) Comité contre l'esclavage moderne, *Les formes contemporaines d'esclavage dans six pays de l'Union Européenne: Autriche, Belgique, Espagne, France, Grande-Bretagne, Italie*, research supported by Daphne Programme, European Commission.

Caldwell, G., Galster, S., and Steinzor, N. (1997) *Crime and Servitude: An Exposé of the Traffic in Women for Prostitution from the Newly Independent States*, Moscow: Global Survival Network.

Cameron S., and Newman E. (2004) 'Trafficking of Filipino Women to Japan: Examining the Experiences and Perspectives of Victims and Government Experts', Executive Summary, United Nations Global Programme against Trafficking in Human Beings, Coalitions against Trafficking in Human Beings in the Philippines, Phase 1.

Campani, G. (1998) 'Trafficking for Sexual Exploitation and the Sex Business in the New Context of International Migration: The Case of Italy', *South European Society & Politics* 3.

Caouette, T., and Saito, Y. (1999) *To Japan and Back: Thai Women Recount Their Experiences*, Geneva: International Organization for Migration.

Carchedi, F., et al. (2000) *I colori della notte. Migrazioni, sfruttamento sessuale, esperienze di intervento sociale*, Milan: Franco Angeli.

Carroll, R. (2000) 'Auctions for Sex: Europe's Thriving Slavery Industry', *Guardian*, 23 May.

Censis (2002) 'Il comportamento sessuale degli italiani', in *Annuario Sociale 2001*, Turin: Edizioni Gruppo Abele.

CICP–UNICRI (1999) Centre for International Crime Prevention, United Nations Interregional Crime and Justice Research Institute, *Global Programme against Trafficking in Human Beings: An Outline for Action*, Vienna.

Cordero, T., Facio, A. (2000) 'Trafficking in Women and Children for the Sex Industry. Women's Participation in this Crime. A Contextual Approach', report to the workshop 'Women in the Criminal Justice System', Tenth United Nations Congress on the Prevention of Crime and the Treatment of Offenders, Vienna, 10–17 April.

Corso, C., and Landi, S. (1998) *Quanto vuoi? Clienti e prostitute si raccontano*, Florence: Giunti.

Council of Europe (2003) 'Group of Specialists on the Impact of the Use of New Technologies on Trafficking in Human Beings for the Purposes of Sexual Exploitation', Final Report (EG-S-NT), Strasbourg, February.

Dal Lago, A. (1998) *The Impact of Migrations on Receiving Societies*, Brussels: European Commission.

Danna, D. (2000) 'La prostituzione di strada nell'Unione Europea: le stime più recenti', *Polis*, vol. 14, no. 2, August.

David, F., and Monzini, P. (2000) 'Human Smuggling and Trafficking:

A Desk Review on the Trafficking in Women from the Philippines', United Nations Interregional Crime and Justice Research Institute and Australian Institute of Criminology, Conference paper for the Tenth UN Congress on the Prevention of Crime and the Treatment of Offenders, Vienna, 10–17 April.

Demleitner, N.V. (1994) 'Forced Prostitution: Naming an International Offence', *Fordham International Law Journal* 18, November.

Demleitner, N.V. (1999) 'Human Trafficking: The Need for Further Research', report to University of Michigan Law School, December.

De Ruyer, B., and Van Impe, K. (2000) 'Trafficking in Women through Poland, Analysis of the Phenomenon, Causes of (Trans)migration and Proposals to Tackle the Problem', Ghent University, paper presented at the workshop 'Women in the Criminal Justice System', Tenth UN Congress on the Prevention of Crime and the Treatment of Offenders, Vienna, 10–17 April.

Doole, C. (2001) 'Albania Blamed for Human Trafficking. Gangs Use Albania to Lure Women into Prostitution', *BBC News*, 17 April.

Dottridge, M. (1999) 'Anti-Slavery International, International Instruments Against Trafficking in Persons: When the Excellent is the Enemy of the Good', paper presented at the NGOs meeting 'Trafficking and the Global Sex Industry: Need for Human Rights Framework', Geneva: Palais des Nations, 21–22 June.

ECPAT (2003) End Child Prostitution, Child Pornography and Trafficking in Children for Sexual Purposes, *Country Profile: Russia*, report available at www.Ecpatnet/eng/Ecpat.

Ehrenreich, B., and Hochschild, A. (2002) *Global Woman: Nannies, Maids and Sex Workers in the New Economy*, New York: Owl Books.

Estes, R.J., and Weiner, N.A. (2001) 'The Commercial Sexual Exploitation of Children in the United States, Canada and Mexico', http://caster.ssw.upenn.edu/~restes/CSEC.htm, September.

Europap/Tampep (2001) European Network for HIV/STD Prevention in Prostitution, *Final Report and Summary 1998–2000*, available at: www.europap.net/final/contents.htm.

European Parliament (2004) Committee on Women's Rights and Equal Opportunities, *Draft Report on the Consequences of the Sex Industry in the European Union*, provisional, 2003/2107(INI) 9 January, Rapporteur M. Eriksson.

Europol (2004) *Trafficking of Human Beings: A Europol Perspective*, report, January.

Foundation of Women's Forum (1999) *Crossing Borders against Trafficking in Women and Girls: A Resource Book for Working against Trafficking in the Baltic Sea Region*, Stockholm.

Ghosh, B. (1998) *Huddled Masses and Uncertain Shores: Insights into Irregular Migration*, The Hague: Kluwer Law International/Martinus Nijhoff Publishers.

Gomez, C.J. (ed.) (2001) *Sex Trafficking of Women in the United States: International and Domestic Trends*, Coalition Against Trafficking in Women, March.

Gorbunova, L. (1999) 'Countering Trafficking in Women and Girls: Regional Cooperation', paper presented at the international conference 'New Frontiers of Crime: Trafficking in Human Beings and New Forms of Slavery', organized by UNICRI, Verona, 22–23 October.

Gramegna, M. (1999) 'Trafficking in Human Beings in Sub-Saharan Africa: the Case of Nigeria', paper presented at the international conference 'New Frontiers of Crime: Trafficking in Human Beings and New Forms of Slavery', organized by UNICRI, Verona, 22–23 October.

Hodgson, D. (1994) 'Sex Tourism and Child Prostitution in Asia: Legal Responses and Strategies', in *Melbourne University Law Review* 19.

Home Office (2004) 'Paying the Price: A Consultation Paper on Prostitution', London: Home Office Communication Directorate, July.

Horbunova, O. (1999) Ukrainian Centre for Women's Studies/International Women's Rights Centre–La Strada, paper presented at the NGO meeting 'Trafficking and the Global Sex Industry: Need for Human Rights Framework', Geneva: Palais des Nations, 21–22 June.

Hughes, D.M. (2000a) '"Welcome to the Rape Camp". Sexual Exploitation and the Internet in Cambodia', paper presented at Rhode Island University.

Hughes, D.M. (2000b) 'The "Natasha" Trade: The Transnational Shadow Trade of Trafficking in Women', *Journal of International Affairs*, special number, *In the Shadows: Promoting Prosperity or Undermining Instability?*, vol. 53, no. 2, Spring: 625–51.

Hughes, D.M. (2000c) 'Men Create the Demand; Women Are the Supply', Conference on Sexual Exploitation, Queen Sofia Centre, Valencia, November.

Hughes, D.M. (2002) *Trafficking for Sexual Exploitation: The Case of the Russian Federation*, IOM, Geneva, www.iom.int//documents/publication/en/mrs_7_2002.pdf.

Hughes, D.M. (2004) 'Best Practices to Address the Demand Side of Sex Trafficking', paper for the Women's Studies Program, University of Rhode Island, August.

Human Rights Watch/Asia (1995) *Rape for Profit: Trafficking of Nepali Girls and Women to India's Brothels*, New York.

Human Rights Watch (2000a) 'International Trafficking of Women and Children', testimony before the Senate Committee on Foreign Relations Subcommittee on Near Eastern and South Asian Affairs, by Regan E. Ralph, Executive Director, Women's Rights Division, February.

Human Rights Watch (2000b) *Owed Justice: Thai Women Trafficked into Debt Bondage in Japan*, New York.

Ibolya, D. (1999) 'Hungary, a Transit Country between East and West: Experiences and Recommendations', paper presented at the international conference 'New Frontiers of Crime: Trafficking in Human Beings and New Forms of Slavery', organized by UNICRI, Verona, 22–23 October.

ILO (2004) International Labour Organization, *Towards a Fair Deal for Migrant Workers in the Global Economy*, Geneva.

IOM (International Organization for Migration) (1995) 'Trafficking and Prostitution: the Growing Exploitation of Migrant Women from Central and Eastern Europe', paper, Migration Information Program, Geneva.

IOM (1996a) 'Trafficking in Women to Austria for Sexual Exploitation', paper, Migration Information Program, Geneva.

IOM (1996b) 'Trafficking in Women from the Dominican Republic for Sexual Exploitation', paper, Migration Information Program, Geneva.

IOM (1997) 'The Baltic Route: The Trafficking of Migrants through Lithuania', paper, Geneva.

IOM (1998) *Information Campaign against Trafficking in Women from Ukraine*, Research Report, July.

IOM (1999) 'Trafficking in Migrants: IOM Policy and Responses', paper, Geneva.

IOM (2001a) 'Trafficking in Unaccompanied Minors for Sexual Exploitation in the European Union', paper, Geneva.

IOM (2001b) 'New IOM Figures on the Global Scale of Trafficking', *Trafficking in Migrants Quarterly Bulletin*, 23, April.

IOM (2001c) *Country Report: Italy, Applied Research and Data Collection on*

Trafficking in Women and Children for Sexual Exploitation to, through and from the Balkan Region, Geneva: ARTB.

IOM (2001d) Rome Mission and Tirana Mission, *Proceedings of the Conference 'The Italy-Albania Counter-trafficking Experience: A Dialogue on Lessons Learned and Future Practices'*, Tirana, 31 October 2000.

IOM (2001e) Pristina Counter-Trafficking Unit 2001, 'The Profile of Women Trafficked into Kosovo Based on a Sample of 130 Assisted Cases from February 2000 to February 15th 2001', Pristina.

IOM (2001f) 'Deceived Migrants from Tajikistan. A Study of Trafficking in Women and Children', Geneva.

IOM (2004a) IOM Counter-Trafficking Center, 'Changing Pattern and Trends of Trafficking in Persons, the Balkan Region', July.

IOM (2004b) Report submitted by J. Engel, MiraMed Institute, to the Office to Monitor and Combat Trafficking in Persons, 'Assisting Victims of Sexual Trafficking to and from the Russian Federation', Year One Final Report, Moscow.

IOM (2004c) Research and Publications Division, 'Human Trafficking: Bibliography by Region', draft paper presented at the International Expert Meeting *Improving Data and Research on Human Trafficking*, Rome, 27–28 May.

Janie, C. (1998) 'Redirecting the Debate over Trafficking in Women: Definitions, Paradigms, and Contexts', *Harvard Human Rights Journal* 11.

Jaschok, M., and Miers, S. (eds) (1994) *Women and Chinese Patriarchy: Submission, Servitude and Escape*, London: Zed Books.

Kane, J. (1998) *Sold for Sex*, Aldershot: Arena.

Kangaspunta, K. (2003) 'Mapping the Inhuman Trade: Preliminary Findings of the Database on Trafficking in Human Beings', *Forum on Crime and Society*, vol. 3, nos 1–2, December: 81–104.

Katharina, K., and Gabriele, R. (1999) *Combat of Trafficking in Women and Forced Prostitution: International Standards*, Vienna: Ludwig Bolzmann Institute of Human Rights.

Kelly, E. (2002) 'Journeys to Jeopardy: Review of Research on Trafficking in Children and Women to Europe', IOM Migration Research Series No. 11, Geneva, November.

Kelly, L., and Regan, L. (2000) 'Stopping Trafficking: Exploring the Extent of, and the Response to Trafficking in Women for Sexual Exploitation', Police Research Series, paper 125, compiled by the University of North London's Child and Woman Abuse Studies Unit,

Home Office Research, Development and Statistics Directorate, London.

Kelly, L. (2002) 'From Rhetoric to Curiosity: Urgent Questions from the UK about Responses to Trafficking in Women', paper for the Child and Women Abuse Studies Unit, University of North London.

Kempadoo, K.J., and Doezema J. (eds) (1998) *Global Sex Workers: Rights, Resistance and Redefinition*, London: Routledge.

Kennedy, I., and Nicotri, P. (1999) *Lucciole nere. Le prostitute nigeriane si raccontano*, Milan: Kaos.

King, G. (2004) *Woman, Child for Sale: The New Slave Trade in the 21st Century*, New York: Chamberlain Bros.

Laczko, F., Stacher, I., and Graf, J. (eds) (1999) International Organization for Migration, International Centre for Migration Policy Development, *Migration in Central and Eastern Europe: 1999 Review*, Geneva.

La Strada (Czech Republic) (1997) 'Traffic in Women in Post-Communist Countries of Central and Eastern Europe', paper.

Lazaroiu, S., and Alexandru, M. (2003) *Who is the Next Victim? Vulnerability of Young Romanian Women to Trafficking in Human Beings*, IOM mission in Romania, Bucharest, August.

Lazos, G. (2000) 'Trafficking and Prostitution in Greece', paper.

Leheny, D. (1995) 'A Political Economy of Asian Sex Tourism', *Annals of Tourism Research*, vol. 22, no. 2.

Lehti M. (2003) 'Trafficking in Women and Children in Europe', HEUNI Paper No. 18, Helsinki: European Institute for Crime Prevention and Control.

Leifholdt, D. (1999) 'The Position Paper of the Coalition against Trafficking in Women', paper presented at the NGOs meeting 'Trafficking and the Global Sex Industry: Need for Human Rights Framework', Geneva: Palais des Nations, 21–22 June.

Leones, C., and Caparas, D. (2002) National Police Commission, Republic of the Philippines, *Trafficking in Human Beings from the Philippines: A Survey of Government Experts and Law Enforcement Case Files*, United Nations Global Programme against Trafficking in Human Beings, Coalitions against Trafficking in Human Beings in the Philippines – Phase 1.

Levchenko, K. (1999) 'Legal Study on the Combat of Trafficking in Women and Forced Prostitution in Ukraine', *Ukraine Country Report*, Vienna: Ludwig Boltzmann Institute of Human Rights.

Leonini, L. (ed.) (1999) *Sesso in acquisto. Una ricerca sui clienti della prostituzione*, Milan: Unicopli.

Levenkron, N., and Dahan, Y. (2003) 'Women as Commodities: Trafficking in Women in Israel', paper prepared for the Hotline for Migrant Workers, Isha L'Isha, Adva Center, Haifa.

Lin, L.L. (ed.) (1998) *The Sex Sector: The Economic and Social Bases of Prostitution in Southeast Asia*, Geneva: International Labour Organization.

Lisborg, A. (2002) 'Bodies across Borders: Prostitution-related Migration from Thailand to Denmark', in, S. Thorbek and B. Pattanaik (eds), *Transnational Prostitution: Changing Global Patterns*, London: Zed Books.

Lloyd, K.A. (2000) 'Wives for Sale: the Modern International Mail Order Bride Industry', *Journal of International Law and Business*, Northwestern School of Law, 20, Winter.

McElroy, W. (2002) *Le gambe della libertà*, Trevilio: Leonardo Flacco Editore.

Malfatti, D., and Tartarini, L. (1998) 'Migrazioni femminili e devianza. Una ricerca sulla prostituzione delle donne immigrate nella città di Genova', *Rassegna italiana di Criminologia* 9.

Mansson, S.A. (2004) 'Men's Practices in Prostitution and their Implications for Social Work', in S.A. Mansson and C. Proveyer (eds), *Social Work in Cuba and Sweden: Achievements and Prospects*, Department of Social Work, Goteborg University and Department of Sociology, University of Havana.

Marcuse, H. (1969) 'Political Preface' (1966), in *Eros and Civilization*, London: Sphere Books.

Mattar, M.Y. (2004) 'The Protection Project of the Johns Hopkins University School of Advanced International Studies: The Scope of the Problem and the Appropriate Responses', paper presented at the Seminar on Globalization and Corruption, Johns Hopkins University, Paul H. Nitze School of Advanced International Studies, 14–15 September.

Mattila, H., Parquet R., and Laczko F. (2004) 'Human Trafficking: A Global Review of Literature', draft paper presented at the International Expert Meeting 'Improving Data and Research on Human Trafficking', organized in Rome by IOM, 27–28 May 2004.

Ministry of Industry, Employment and Communications of Sweden (2004) 'Prostitution and Trafficking in Women', fact sheet, January.

Mira Med Institute (1999) 'Preliminary Survey Report on Sexual Trafficking from the CIS Countries', at www.miramedinstitute.org/trafficking.eng.htlm.

Monzini, P. (1999) *Gruppi criminali a Napoli e a Marsiglia. La delinquenza organizzata nella storia di due città, 1820–1990*, Catanzaro: Meridiana Libri.

Monzini, P. (2004) 'Trafficking in Women and Girls and the Involvement of Organized Crime in Western and Central Europe', *International Review of Criminology* 11: 73–88.

Monzini, P., Pastore, F., and Sciortino, G. (2003) 'The Promised Land: the Organisation of Migrant Trafficking into Italy', Cespi, Centro Studi Politica Internazionale, working paper, Rome.

Muntarbhorn, V. (1996) *Sexual Exploitation of Children*, New York: United Nations Human Rights Center.

Mushakoji, K. (1999) 'The Anatomy of Global Sex Industry: The Political Economy of Human Rights Violations', paper presented at the NGOs meeting 'Trafficking and the Global Sex Industry: Need for Human Rights Framework', Palais des Nations, Geneva, 21–22 June.

Ndiaye, N. (1999) Paper presented at the conference 'Gender Mainstreaming: A Step into the 21st Century', organized by the Council of Europe, Athens, 16–18 September.

Nurmi, R. (2000) 'Mobile Russian Prostitution in Finland', paper presented at the workshop 'Women in the Criminal Justice System', Tenth UN Congress on the Prevention of Crime and the Treatment of Offenders, Vienna, 10–17 April.

O'Connell Davidson, J. (1996) 'Sex Tourism in Cuba', *Race & Class*, vol. 38, no. 1.

O'Connell Davidson, J. (1998) *Prostitution, Power and Freedom*, Cambridge: Polity Press.

O'Connell Davidson, J., and Taylor, S.J. (1994) *Sex Tourism – Thailand, Bangkok*, End Child Prostitution, Child Pornography and the Trafficking of Children for Sexual Purposes (ECPAT).

Ofuoku, M. (1999) 'Sex Export: Dirty Details of Young Nigerian Girls Being Sent to Europe for Prostitution', *Newswatch, Nigeria's Weekly Newsmagazine*, 27 July.

O'Grady, R. (1992) *The Child and the Tourist: The Story behind the Escalation of Child Prostitution in Asia*, Bangkok: ECPAT/Auckland: Pace Publishing.

Olateru-Olagbegi, B. (1999) *The Modern Slavery: The Social and Legal Implications of Trafficking in Women & Children in Nigeria*, Lagos: Women's Consortium of Nigeria (WOCON).

O'Neill-Richard, A. (2000) *International Trafficking in Women in the United States: A Contemporary Manifestation of Slavery and Organized Crime*, DCI

Exceptional Intelligence Analyst Program, Center for the Study of Intelligence, Central Intelligence Agency, Washington.

OSCE (1999) Organization for Security and Cooperation in Europe, *Action Plan for the Year 2000 to Combat Trafficking in Persons in the OSCE Region*, Office for Democratic Institutions and Human Rights, Warsaw.

OSCE (2001) *Trafficking in Human Beings: Implications for the OSCE*, Office for Democratic Institutions and Human Rights, Warsaw.

OSCE (2002) Country reports submitted to the Informal Group on Gender Inequality and Anti-Trafficking in Human Beings, Human Dimension Implementation Meeting, September, Warsaw.

OSCE (2003) *First Annual Report on Victims of Trafficking in South Eastern Europe*, Regional Clearing Point, Task Force on Trafficking in Human Beings, Stability Pact for South Eastern Europe, Vienna.

Pederson, K. (1994) 'Prostitution or Sex Work in the Common Market?', *International Journal of Health Services*, vol. 24, no. 4.

Phongpaichit, P. (1982) *From Peasant Girls to Bangkok Masseuses*, Bangkok: ILO.

Phongpaichit, P., Piriyarangsan, S., and Treerat, N. (1998) *Guns, Girls, Gambling, Ganja: Thailand's Illegal Economy*, Bangkok: Silkworm Books.

Prina, F. (2003) *Trade and Exploitation of Minors and Young Nigerian Women for Prostitution in Italy, Action Programme against the Traffic from Nigeria to Italy of Minors and Young Women for Sexual Exploitation*, Research Report, Turin: UNICRI.

Protection Project (2002a) 'Russia', *A Human Rights Report on Trafficking of Persons, Especially Women and Children*, March: 453–9.

Protection Project (2002b) 'Thailand', *A Human Rights Report on Trafficking of Persons, Especially Women and Children*, March: 535–45.

Protection Project (2002c) 'United Kingdom', *A Human Rights Report on Trafficking of Persons, Especially Women and Children*, March: 575–80.

Protection Project (2002d) 'United States of America', *A Human Rights Report on Trafficking of Persons, Especially Women and Children*, March.

Raymond J.G. (2002) *A Comparative Study of Women Trafficked in the Migration Process: Patterns, Profiles and Health Consequences of Sexual Exploitation in Five Countries (Indonesia, the Philippines, Thailand, Venezuela and the United States)*, Coalition Against Trafficking in Women, www.catwinternational.org.

Raymond, J.G., and Hughes, D. (2001) *Sex Trafficking of Women in the United States: International and Domestic Trends*, Coalition Against Trafficking in Women, www.catwinternational.org.

Redo, S. (2000) 'Migrant Trafficking and Organized Crime', paper, United Nations Office for Drug Control and Crime Prevention (UNDCP), Centre for International Crime Prevention (CICP), Regional Bureau for Central Asia, Tashkent, Uzbekistan.

Renton, D. (2001) *Child Trafficking in Albania*, London: Save the Children.

Ruggiero, V. (1997) 'Trafficking in Human Beings: Slaves in Contemporary Europe', *International Journal of the Sociology of Law* 25.

Salt, J. (1998) Paper presented at the conference on Migrant Trafficking, organized by the International Organization for Migration, Warsaw, 8–9 June.

Salt, J. (2000) 'Trafficking and Human Smuggling: A European Perspective', *International Migration*, vol. 38, no. 3.

Salt, J., and Hogarth, J. (2000) 'Migrant Trafficking and Human Smuggling in Europe: A Review of the Evidence', in F. Laczko and D. Thompson (eds), *Migrant Trafficking and Human Smuggling in Europe: A Review of the Evidence with Case Studies from Hungary, Poland and Ukraine*, Geneva: International Organization for Migration.

Salt, J., and Stein, J. (1997) 'Migration as a Business: The Case of Trafficking', *International Migration*, vol. 35, no. 4.

Scambler, G., and Scambler, A. (1997) *Rethinking Prostitution: Purchasing Sex in the 1990s*, London: Routledge.

Schloenhardt, A. (2000) 'Organized Crime and the Business of Migrant Trafficking: An Economic Analysis', *Crime, Law and Social Change* 32.

Seabrook, J. (1996) *Travels in the Skin Trade: Tourism and the Sex Industry*, London: Pluto Press.

Segre, S. (2000) 'La prostituzione come costruzione sociale e l'identità delle prostitute straniere in Italia', *Quaderni di sociologia*, vol. 14, no. 22.

Shelley, L. (2000) 'Trafficking and Organized Crime', paper presented at Protection Project Seminar Series, American University, 4 October.

Shelley, L. (2003) 'Trafficking in Women: The Business Model Approach', *Brown Journal of World Affairs*, vol. 10, no. 1, Summer/Fall: 119–31.

Simmel, G. (1968) *The Conflict in Modern Culture, and Other Essays*, trs. and ed. Peter Etzkorn, New York: Teachers College Press.

Simmel, G. (1984) *Georg Simmel on Women, Sexuality, and Love*, trans. and ed. Guy Oakes, New Haven: Yale University Press.

Siron, N., and Van Baeveghem, P. (1999) 'Trafficking in Migrants through Poland. Multidisciplinary research into the phenomenon of transit migration in the candidate Member States of the EU, with a view to the combat of traffic in persons', European Commission (STOP), University of Ghent, Maklu, Antwerp/Apeldoorn.

Sita, N.M. (2003) 'Trafficking in Women and Children: Situation and Some Trends in African Countries', report, UNAFRI, May.

Skeldon, R. (2000) 'Trafficking: A Perspective from Asia', *International Migration*, vol. 38, no. 3.

Sleightholme, C., and Sinha, I. (1996) *Guilty without Trial: Women in the Sex Trade in Calcutta*, New Brunswick, NJ: Rutgers University Press.

Southeast Asia Watch (1998) *Roadmap on Migration of Women and Trafficking in Women in Southeast Asia*, Quezon: SEAwatch.

Stalker, P. (2000) *Workers without Frontiers: The Impact of Globalization on International Migration*, Geneva: International Labour Organization.

Stienstra, D. (1996) 'Madonna/Whore, Pimp/Protector: International Law and Organization Related to Prostitution', *Studies in Political Economy* 51, Fall.

Sturdevant Pollock, S., and Stoltzfus, B. (1992) *Let the Good Times Roll: Prostitution and the U.S. Military in Asia*, New York: New Press.

Talens, C. (2001) 'Esclavitud Moderna en España', *La Vanguardia*, 14 July.

Task Force on Organized Crime in the Baltic States (2000) 'Report on the "Fact-finding Mission" Conducted by the National Commissioner of Police for the Baltic Countries', National Commissioner of Danish Police Force Department, November.

Taylor, I., and Jamieson, R. (1999) 'Market Culture: Challenges to Organized Crime Analysis', paper presented at the international conference 'New Frontiers of Crime: Trafficking in Human Beings and New Forms of Slavery', organized by UNICRI, Verona, 22–23 October.

Taylor, I., and Jamieson, R. (1999a) 'Sex Trafficking and the Mainstream of Market Culture', *Crime, Law & Social Change* 32.

Terres des Hommes, Netherlands (2001) 'Summary of a Nation-wide Investigation into Trafficking of Nigerian Under-age Girls into the Netherlands', paper.

Thorbek, S., and Pattanaik, B. (2002) *Transnational Prostitution: Changing Global Patterns*, London: Zed Books.

Trafficking Watch (2004) Issue 5, Summer, International Rescue Committee, available at www.theirc.org.

Transcrime (2003) 'The Organized Crime Situation in the SEE Countries and the Illicit Activities Perpetrated by Organized Criminal Groups', Interim Report for the Office of the Special Coordinator of the Stability Pact for South Eastern Europe, January.

Trends in Organized Crime (1998) *Special Focus on Modern Slavery: Trafficking in Women and Children*, Summer, vol. 3, 4.

UNDP (1999) *Human Development Report 1999*, New York: United Nations Development Program.

UNDP (2000) *Country Report: Nigeria*, New York: United Nations Development Program.

UNICEF (2002) *Trafficking in Human Beings in South-Eastern Europe*, report, Belgrade.

UNICRI (1999) United Nations Interregional Crime and Justice Research Institute, proceedings of the international conference 'New Frontiers of Crime: Trafficking in Human Beings and New Forms of Slavery', organized by UNICRI, Verona, 22–23 October.

UNICRI (2003a) 'Programme of Action against Trafficking in Minors and Young Women from Nigeria into Italy for the Purpose of Sexual Exploitation', desk review.

UNICRI (2003b) *Programme of Action against Trafficking in Minors and Young Women from Nigeria into Italy for the Purpose of Sexual Exploitation*, Report of Field Survey in Edo State, Nigeria.

United Nations (2000) *Protocol to Prevent, Suppress and Punish Trafficking in Persons, Especially Women and Children*, supplementing the United Nations Convention against Transnational Organized Crime, www.uncjin.org/Documents/Conventions/dcatoc/final_documents_2/convention_%20traff_eng.pdf.

UNODC (2003) United Nations Office for Drug Control and Crime Prevention, *Coalitions against Trafficking in Human Beings in the Philippines, Research and Action*, Final Report.

UNODC (2004a) *Global Programme against Trafficking in Human Beings: The Case of Czech Republic*, report, Vienna.

UNODC (2004b) *The Case of Poland*, report, Vienna.

UK Government (2004) *Trafficking in the UK, Crime Reduction Toolkits*, available at www.crimereduction.gov.uk/toolkits/tp0102.htm.

US Department of State (2004) Office to Monitor and Combat Trafficking in Persons, *Trafficking in Persons Report*, Washington, DC, available at www.state.gov/g/tip/rls/tiprp/2004.

Vandeckerckhove W., Pari, Z., Moens, B., Orfano, I., Hopkins, R., Njiboer, N., Vermeulen, G., and Bontinck, W. (2003) 'Research Based on Case Studies of Victims of Trafficking in Human Beings in 3 EU Member States, i.e. Belgium, Italy and the Netherlands', Payoke – On the Road – De Rode Draad, European Commission: University of Ghent.

Viviano, F. (2001) 'New Mafias Go Global: High-tech Trade in Humans and Drugs', *San Francisco Chronicle*, 7 January.

Vocks, J., and Nijboer, J. (2000) 'The Promised Land: A Study of Trafficking in Women from Central and Eastern Europe in the Netherlands', paper.

Weltzer-Lang, D., Barbosa, O., Mathieu, I. (1994) 'Prostitution: les uns, les unes et les autres', Paris: Editions Métaillié.

Wijers, M. (1998) 'Women, Labor, and Migration: The Position of Trafficked Women and Strategies for Support', in K.J. Kempadoo and J. Doezema (eds), *Global Sex Workers: Rights, Resistance and Redefinition*, London: Routledge.

Wijers, M., and Lap-Chew, L. (1997) *Trafficking in Women: Forced Labour and Slavery-Like Practices in Marriage, Domestic Labour and Prostitution*, Anraad, Foundation Against Trafficking in Women and Global Alliance Against Traffic in Women.

Williams, P. (1997) 'Trafficking in Women and Children: A Market Perspective', *Transnational Organized Crime*, vol. 3, no. 4.

Wolthius, A., Blaak, M. (eds) (2002) 'Trafficking in Children for Sexual Purposes from Eastern Europe to Western Europe. An Explanatory Research in Eight Western European Receiving Countries', ECPAT Europe, Law Enforcement Group, Amsterdam.

Italian judicial documentation

Procura Distrettuale Antimafia, L'Aquila (1999) Operazione Aranit, Informativa, 2° parte, Lo sfruttamento e favoreggiamento della prostituzione, procedimento n. 15/99 RGNR PD.

Procura Distrettuale Antimafia, L'Aquila (2000) Richiesta per l'applicazione di misure cautelari, n. 15/99, 30 giugno, RGNR PD.

Questura di Udine (2000) Annotazione finale sulla Mafia Nigeriana, Operazione Edo, 8 novembre.

Tribunale dell'Aquila (2000) Tribunale dell'Aquila, Ufficio del Giudice per le Indagini Preliminari di competenza distrettuale, Ordinanza contro Ago Perparim+70, 9 giugno.

Tribunale di Lecce (1997) Procura della Repubblica presso il Tribunale di Lecce, Direzione Distrettuale Antimafia, Decreto di fermo nei confronti di Capi Erion+15, n. 2800/97 RGNR, n. 113/97 RDDA, 25 novembre.

Tribunale di Lecce (1999a) Ufficio del Pubblico Ministero presso il Tribunale di Lecce, 3 verbali di denuncia orale, Regione dei Carabinieri Puglia, Stazione di Otranto, procedimento n. 3367/99 RGNR.

Tribunale di Lecce (1999b) Ufficio del Pubblico Ministero presso il Tribunale di Lecce, 2 verbali di altre sommarie informazioni, Guardia di Finanza, 17° Legione della Guardia di Finanza, procedimento n. 3392/99 RGNR.

Tribunale di Lecce (2000a) Verbale di incidente probatorio, procedimento a carico di Hoxhallari Vicktor, n. 4367/2000 RGGIP, 9 novembre.

Tribunale di Lecce (2000b) Verbale di udienza, procedimento a carico di Indrisllari Albert+1, n. 581/2000 RGT Nuovo Rito, 5321/2000 RGPM NR.

Tribunale di Lecce (2000c) Verbale di denuncia-querela, Regione dei Carabinieri Puglia, procedimento n. 2367/00 RGNR.

Tribunale di Lecce (2000d) Verbale di ricezione di denuncia, Regione dei Carabinieri Puglia, procedimento n. 5074/00 RGNR.

Tribunale di Lecce (2000e) Verbale di querela, Regione dei Carabinieri Puglia, procedimento n. 5580/00 RGNR.

Tribunale di Lecce (2000f) Verbale di denuncia, Regione dei Carabinieri Puglia, procedimento n. 6235/00 RGNR.

Tribunale di Lecce (2000g) Verbale di ricezione di denuncia, Regione Carabinieri Puglia, procedimento penale n. 4449/00 RGNR.

Tribunale di Lecce (2000h) Verbale di sommarie informazioni testimoniali, Questura di Lecce, procedimento n. 2868/00 RGNR.

Tribunale di Lecce (2000i) 2 verbali di denuncia per sfruttamento della prostituzione, Questura di Lecce, procedimento n. 2868/00 RGNR.

Tribunale di Lecce (2000l) 4 verbali di 'altre sommarie informazioni', Guardia di Finanza, procedimento n. 5321/00 RGNR.

Tribunale di Lecce (2001a) Verbale di denuncia, Questura di Lecce, procedimento n. 8362/01 RGNR.

Tribunale di Lecce (2001b) Verbale di udienza preliminare, procedimento contro Krusa Sadete+1, n. 5580/2000 RGNR, n. 3868/2000 RGGIP.

Tribunale di Milano (1999a) Procura della Repubblica presso il Tribunale di Milano, Verbali di interrogatorio di persone sottoposte ad indagini, e Verbali di assunzioni di informazioni, procedimento n. 11969/98 R.G., 5 maggio.

Tribunale di Milano (1999b) Richiesta di rinvio a giudizio di Robert Spahiu+4, procedimento n. 5692/99 RGNR – Mod. 21, 19 giugno.

Tribunale di Milano (1999c) Ufficio del Giudice delle indagini preliminari del Tribunale di Milano, decreto che dispone il giudizio di Rex-hepi Kujtim+2, n. 5692 RGNR, n. 3282 RGGIP, 6 luglio.

Tribunale di Milano (1999d) Sentenza contro Robert Spahiu e Artian Spahiu, 6 luglio.

Tribunale di Padova (1997) Procura della Repubblica presso il Tribunale di Padova, procedimento a carico di Okoye Paulinus+23, n. 2272/97 RGNR.

Tribunale di Reggio Calabria (2002) Ufficio del giudice per le indagini preliminari, ordinanza per l'applicazione di misure cautelari n. 1219/01 R.G.N.R., n. 6614/01 R.G. GIP, n. 18/02 00 CC, 3 aprile.

Tribunale di Trento (1999) Ufficio del Giudice per le indagini preliminari, Ordinanza di custodia cautelare in carcere nei confronti di Aniugbo Justina+44, Nr. 247/97 r.g. notizie di reato – 1/97 D.D.A., 23

Websites

International NGOs and projects

Anti-Slavery International: www.antislavery.org.

Coalition Against Trafficking in Women: www.catwinternational.org.

Human Rights Watch: www.hrw.org/about/projects/traffcamp/intro.html.

Global Alliance against Traffic in Women: www.inet.co.th/org/gaatw.

End Child Prostitution, Child Pornography and Trafficking in Children: www.ecpat.it.

Florida Freedom: www.floridafreedom.org.

Humantrafficking.org: www.humantrafficking.org.

Protection Project: www.protectionreport.org (country reports).

Q Web, Women's Empowerment Base: www.qweb.kvinnoforum.se/.

Stop-traffic listserver: www.friends-partners.org/pipermail/stop-traffic/2004/000113.html.

Inter-governmental organizations

International Organization for Migration: www.iom.int.

International Labour Organization: www.ilo.org.

Office of the United Nations High Commissioner for Human Rights: www.ohchr.org/english/issues/trafficking/index.htm.

United Nations Office on Drugs and Crime: www.unodc.org/odccp/trafficking_human_beings.html.

United Nations Interregional Crime and Justice Research Institute: www. unicri.it.

United Nations Development Fund for Women, South Asia Regional Anti-trafficking Program: www.unifemantitrafficking.org/main.html.

Organization for Security and Co-operation in Europe: www.osce.org/ odihr/?page=democratization&div=antitrafficking.

South East European Regional Initiative Against Human Trafficking: www.seerights.org/.

Council of Europe: www.coe.int/T/E/human_rights/trafficking.

European Commission: www.europa.eu.int.

Governmental agencies

US Department of State: www.state.gov/g/tip/.

UK Home Office: www.crimereduction.gov.uk/toolkits/tp0102.htm.

Index

About this series

'Communities in the South are facing great difficulties in coping with global trends. I hope this brave new series will throw much needed light on the issues ahead and help us choose the right options.'

MARTIN KHOR, *Director,*
Third World Network, Penang

'There is no more important campaign than our struggle to bring the global economy under democratic control. But the issues are fearsomely complex. This Global Issues series is a valuable resource for the committed campaigner and the educated citizen.'

BARRY COATES,
Director, Oxfam New Zealand

'Zed Books has long provided an inspiring list about the issues that touch and change people's lives. The Global Issues series is another dimension of Zed's fine record, allowing access to a range of subjects and authors that, to my knowledge, very few publishers have tried. I strongly recommend these new, powerful titles and this exciting series.'

JOHN PILGER, *author*

'We are all part of a generation that actually has the means to eliminate extreme poverty world-wide. Our task is to harness the forces of globalization for the benefit of working people, their families and their communities – that is our collective duty. The Global Issues series makes a powerful contribution to the global campaign for justice, sustainable and equitable development, and peaceful progress.'

GLENYS KINNOCK, *MEP*

The Global Issues series

Already available

Peggy Antrobus, *The Global Women's Movement: Origins, Issues and Strategies*

Walden Bello, *Deglobalization: Ideas for a New World Economy*

Robert Ali Brac de la Perrière and Franck Seuret, *Brave New Seeds: The Threat of GM Crops to Farmers*

Greg Buckman, *Globalization: Tame it or Scrap It?*

Greg Buckman, *Global Trade: Past Mistakes, Future Choices*

Ha-Joon Chang and Ilene Grabel, *Reclaiming Development: An Alternative Economic Policy Manual*

Koen De Feyter, *Human Rights: Social Justice in the Age of the Market*

Oswaldo de Rivero, *The Myth of Development: The Non-viable Economies of the 21st Century*

Graham Dunkley, *Free Trade: Myth, Reality and Alternatives*

Joyeeta Gupta, *Our Simmering Planet: What to Do about Global Warming?*

Nicholas Guyatt, *Another American Century? The United States and the World since 9/11*

Ann-Christin Sjölander Holland, *Water for Sale? Corporations against People*

Martin Khor, *Rethinking Globalization: Critical Issues and Policy Choices*

John Madeley, *Food for All: The Need for a New Agriculture*

John Madeley, *Hungry for Trade: How the Poor Pay for Free Trade*

Damien Millet and Eric Toussaint, *Who Owes Who? 50 Questions About World Debt*

Paola Monzini, *Sex Traffic: Prostitution, Crime and Exploitation*

A.G. Noorani, *Islam and Jihad: Prejudice versus Reality*

Riccardo Petrella, *The Water Manifesto: Arguments for a World Water Contract*

Peter Robbins, *Stolen Fruit: The Tropical Commodities Disaster*

Toby Shelley, *Oil: Politics, Poverty and the Planet*

Vandana Shiva, *Protect or Plunder? Understanding Intellectual Property Rights*

Harry Shutt, *A New Democracy: Alternatives to a Bankrupt World Order*

David Sogge, *Give and Take: What's the Matter with Foreign Aid?*

Paul Todd and Jonathan Bloch, *Global Intelligence: The World's Secret Services Today*

In preparation

Liz Kelly, *Violence against Women*

Alan Marshall, *A New Nuclear Age? The Case for Nuclear Power Revisited*

Roger Moody, *Digging the Dirt: The Modern World of Global Mining*

Jonathon W. Moses, *International Migration: Globalization's Last Frontier*

Edgar Pieterse, *City Futures: Confronting the Crisis of Urban Development*

Peter M. Rosset, *Food is Not Just Another Commodity: Why the WTO Should Get Out of Agriculture*

Toby Shelley, *Nanotechnology: New Promises, New Dangers*

Vivien Stern, *The Making of Crime: Prisons and People in a Market Society*

For full details of this list and Zed's other subject and general catalogues, please write to: The Marketing Department, Zed Books, 7 Cynthia Street, London NI 9JF, UK or email Sales@zedbooks.net

Visit our website at: www.zedbooks.co.uk

Participating organizations

Both ENDS A service and advocacy organization which collaborates with environment and indigenous organizations, both in the South and in the North, with the aim of helping to create and sustain a vigilant and effective environmental movement.

Nieuwe Keizersgracht 45, 1018 VC Amsterdam, The Netherlands
Phone: +31 20 623 0823   Fax: +31 20 620 8049
Email: info@bothends.org   Website: www.bothends.org

Catholic Institute for International Relations (CIIR) CIIR aims to contribute to the eradication of poverty through a programme that combines advocacy at national and international level with community-based development.

Unit 3, Canonbury Yard, 190a New North Road, London N1 7BJ, UK
Phone +44 (0)20 7354 0883   Fax +44 (0)20 7359 0017
Email: ciir@ciir.org   Website: www.ciir.org

Corner House The Corner House is a UK-based research and solidarity group working on social and environmental justice issues in North and South.

PO Box 3137, Station Road, Sturminster Newton, Dorset DT10 1YJ, UK
Tel.: +44 (0)1258 473795   Fax: +44 (0)1258 473748
Email: cornerhouse@gn.apc.org   Website: www.cornerhouse.icaap.org

Council on International and Public Affairs (CIPA) CIPA is a human rights research, education and advocacy group, with a particular focus on economic and social rights in the USA and elsewhere around the world. Emphasis in recent years has been given to resistance to corporate domination.

777 United Nations Plaza, Suite 3C, New York, NY 10017, USA
Tel. +1 212 972 9877   Fax +1 212 972 9878
Email: cipany@igc.org   Website: www.cipa-apex.org

Dag Hammarskjöld Foundation The Dag Hammarskjöld Foundation, established 1962, organises seminars and workshops on social, economic and cultural issues facing developing countries with a particular focus on alternative and innovative solutions. Results are published in its journal *Develpment Dialogue.*

Övre Slottsgatan 2, 753 10 Uppsala, Sweden.
Tel.: +46 18 102772   Fax: +46 18 122072
Email: secretariat@dhf.uu.se   Website: www.dhf.uu.se

Development GAP   The Development Group for Alternative Policies is a Non-Profit Development Resource Organization working with popular organizations in the South and their Northern partners in support of a development that is truly sustainable and that advances social justice.

927 15th Street NW, 4th Floor, Washington, DC, 20005, USA
Tel.: +1 202 898 1566   Fax: +1 202 898 1612
E-mail: dgap@igc.org   Website: www.developmentgap.org

Focus on the Global South   Focus is dedicated to regional and global policy analysis and advocacy work. It works to strengthen the capacity of organizations of the poor and marginalized people of the South and to better analyse and understand the impacts of the globalization process on their daily lives.

C/o CUSRI, Chulalongkorn University, Bangkok 10330, Thailand
Tel.: +66 2 218 7363 Fax: +66 2 255 9976
Email: Admin@focusweb.org   Website: www.focusweb.org

IBON   IBON Foundation is a research, education and information institution that provides publications and services on socio-economic issues as support to advocacy in the Philippines and abroad. Through its research and databank, formal and non-formal education programmes, media work and international networking, IBON aims to build the capacity of both Philippine and international organizations.

Room 303 SCC Bldg, 4427 Int. Old Sta. Mesa, Manila 1008, Philippines
Phone +632 7132729   Fax +632 7160108
Email: editors@ibon.org   Website: www.ibon.org

Inter Pares   Inter Pares, a Canadian social justice organization, has been active since 1975 in building relationships with Third World development groups and providing support for community-based development programmes. Inter Pares is also involved in education and advocacy in Canada, promoting understanding about the causes, effects and solutions to poverty.

221 Laurier Avenue East, Ottawa, Ontario, KIN 6P1 Canada
Phone +1 613 563 4801   Fax +1 613 594 4704
Email: info@interpares.ca   Website: www.interpares.ca

Public Interest Research Centre   PIRC is a research and campaigning group based in Delhi which seeks to serve the information needs of activists and organizations working on macro-economic issues concerning finance, trade and development.

142 Maitri Apartments, Plot No. 28, Patparganj, Delhi 110092, India
Phone: +91 11 2221081/2432054   Fax: +91 11 2224233
Email: kaval@nde.vsnl.net.in

Third World Network TWN is an international network of groups and individuals involved in efforts to bring about a greater articulation of the needs and rights of peoples in the Third World; a fair distribution of the world's resources; and forms of development which are ecologically sustainable and fulfil human needs. Its international secretariat is based in Penang, Malaysia.

121-S Jalan Utama, 10450 Penang, Malaysia
Tel.: +60 4 226 6159   Fax: +60 4 226 4505
Email: twnet@po.jaring.my   Website: www.twnside.org.sg

Third World Network–Africa TWN–Africa is engaged in research and advocacy on economic, environmental and gender issues. In relation to its current particular interest in globalization and Africa, its work focuses on trade and investment, the extractive sectors and gender and economic reform.

2 Ollenu Street, East Legon, PO Box AN19452, Accra-North, Ghana.
Tel.: +233 21 511189/503669/500419   Fax: +233 21 511188
Email: twnafrica@ghana.com

World Development Movement (WDM) The World Development Movement campaigns to tackle the causes of poverty and injustice. It is a democratic membership movement that works with partners in the South to cancel unpayable debt and break the ties of IMF conditionality, for fairer trade and investment rules, and for strong international rules on multinationals.

25 Beehive Place, London SW9 7QR, UK
Tel.: +44 (0)20 7737 6215   Fax: +44 (0)20 7274 8232
Email: wdm@wdm.org.uk   Website: www.wdm.org.uk

This book is also available
in the following countries

CARIBBEAN

Arawak Publications
17 Kensington Crescent
Apt 5
Kingston 5, Jamaica
Tel: 876 960 7538
Fax: 876 960 9219

EGYPT

MERIC
2 Bahgat Ali Street,
Tower D/Apt. 24
Zamalek, Cairo
Tel: 20 2 735 3818/3824
Fax: 20 2 736 9355

FIJI

University Book Centre,
University of South Pacific
Suva
Tel: 679 313 900
Fax: 679 303 265

GHANA

Readwide Books Ltd
12 Ablade Road
Kanda Estates, Kanda
Accra, Ghana
Tel: 233 244 630 805
Tel: 233 208 180 310

GUYANA

Austin's Book Services
190 Church St
Cummingsburg
Georgetown
austins@guyana.net.gy
Tel: 592 227 7395
Fax: 592 227 7396

IRAN

Book City
743 North Hafez Avenue
15977 Tehran

Tel: 98 21 889 7875
Fax: 98 21 889 7785
bookcity@neda.net

MAURITIUS

Editions Le Printemps
4 Club Rd, Vacoas

MOZAMBIQUE

Sul Sensações
PO Box 2242, Maputo
Tel: 258 1 421974
Fax: 258 1 423414

NAMIBIA

Book Den
PO Box 3469, Shop 4
Frans Indongo Gardens
Windhoek
Tel: 264 61 239976
Fax: 264 61 234248

NEPAL

Everest Media Services,
GPO Box 5443
Dillibazar
Putalisadak Chowk
Kathmandu
Tel: 977 1 416026
Fax: 977 1 250176

NIGERIA

Mosuro Publishers
52 Magazine Road
Jericho, Ibadan
Tel: 234 2 241 3375
Fax: 234 2 241 3374

PAKISTAN

Vanguard Books
45 The Mall,
Lahore
Tel: 92 42 735 5079
Fax: 92 42 735 5197

PAPUA NEW GUINEA

Unisearch PNG Pty Ltd
Box 320, University
National Capital District
Tel: 675 326 0130
Fax: 675 326 0127

RWANDA

Librairie Ikirezi
PO Box 443, Kigali
Tel/Fax: 250 71314

SUDAN

The Nile Bookshop
New Extension Street 41
PO Box 8036, Khartoum
Tel: 249 11 463 749

TANZANIA

TEMA Publishing Co Ltd
PO Box 63115
Dar Es Salaam
Tel: 255 51 113608
Fax: 255 51 110472

UGANDA

Aristoc Booklex Ltd
PO Box 5130, Kampala Rd
Diamond Trust Building
Kampala
Tel/Fax: 256 41 254867

ZAMBIA

UNZA Press
PO Box 32379, Lusaka
Tel: 260 1 290409
Fax: 260 1 253952

ZIMBABWE

Weaver Press
PO Box A1922
Avondale, Harare
Tel: 263 4 308330
Fax: 263 4 339645